crochet
dress-up

crochet
dress-up

over **35** cute and easy pieces to create character costumes

Emma Friedlander-Collins

CICO BOOKS
LONDON NEW YORK

In memory of Claire Richardson

Published in 2015 by CICO Books
An imprint of Ryland Peters & Small Ltd
20–21 Jockey's Fields   341 E 116th St
London WC1R 4BW   New York, NY 10029

www.rylandpeters.com

10 9 8 7 6 5 4 3 2 1

ISBN UK: 978-1-78249-195-8
ISBN US: 978-1-78249-212-2

Printed in China

Editor: Rachel Atkinson
Designer: Barbara Zuniga
Photographer: Terry Benson
Stylist: Robert Merrett
Illustrator: Stephen Dew

Art Director: Sally Powell
Production: Meskerem Berhane
Publishing Manager: Penny Craig
Publisher: Cindy Richards

Contents

Introduction   6
Before you begin   8

Pete the Pirate 12
Beard 14
Eye patch 15
Tricorn hat 16
Skull and crossbones motif 19
Parrot 20

Little Mermaid 22
Hair 25
Tail 26
Little crab 28

Superhero 30
Mask 32
Star motif 33
Cuffs 35
Chest plate 37

Snow Queen 38
Snowflake crown 40
Snowflake collar 43
Icicle cuffs 44

Robin Hood 46
Hat 48
Arrow quiver 51
Wrist guards 53

Forest Fairy 54
Flower garland 56
Corsage 59
Fairy wings 60

Cowboy Carl (or Carla) 62
Hat 64
Holster 66
Sheriff's badge 68

Red Riding Hood 70
Hooded cape 72
Basket 74
Apple 76

Pussy Cat 78
Hat 80
Tail 81

Magic Unicorn 82
Horn headdress 84
Tail 85

Vigo the Viking 86
Helmet 89
Thor's hammer 90
Viking cuffs 93

Rapunzel 94
Hair 96
Shrug 99

Wicked Witch 100
Hat 102
Cobweb collar 104
Spider 106

Wily Wizard 108
Hat and stars 110
Beard 112

Grey Rabbit 114
Hat 116
Tail 117

Techniques 118
Conversion chart 126
Suppliers 126
Index 127
Acknowledgments 128

Introduction

Once upon a time there was a craftaholic who loved all textiles, and spent all her free time wandering around haberdashers and yarn shops, mooning over the beautiful things. Now, when she was young she'd been taught how to knit, and she was just horrible at it. No matter how hard she tried or how much she practiced, she just couldn't help dropping stitches, adding stitches, and getting terribly muddled when it came to reading patterns, so she gave it up as a lost cause, but carried on mooning over yarn all the while.

One day, shortly after her first "little beast" was born, she was struck by the fact that she had never considered crochet. One hook, one ball of yarn, and some online tutorials later, an addiction was born. Desperate to make some super-cute and über-cool things for her little one to dress up in, she searched and searched but couldn't find anything to make, so she started designing her own pieces and writing her own patterns. With some gentle encouragement from her beloved, a little Etsy shop was set up under the name of "Steel & Stitch" and the patterns started selling worldwide.

This book is a collection of my original dressing-up pieces, all made for my sons—now big beast and little beast—their friends, and my nephews (and me, sometimes). The originals have all been worn many times, but because of the wonder of crochet they hold their shape, are soft enough for even the littlest ones, can be washed (VERY important if your beasts are anything like mine), and can mostly be made in a couple of hours.

Before you begin

Here are a few things you need to know, and equipment you will need, before you start to crochet.

ABBREVIATIONS

ch(s)	Chain(s)
ch-sp	Chain space
cm	Centimetre
dc	Double crochet
dc2tog	Double crochet 2 stitches together to decrease 1 stitch
dtr	Double treble crochet
g	Gram
htr	Half treble crochet
in	Inches
m	Metre
mm	Millimetre
oz	Ounce
pm	Place markert
rep	Repeat
RS	Right side of work
ss	Slip stitch
st(s)	Stitch(es)
tr	Treble crochet
tr2tog	Treble crochet 2 stitches together to decrease 1 stitch
trtr	Triple treble crochet
t-ch	Turning chain
WS	Wrong side of work
yds	Yards

EQUIPMENT

Craft wire: Used to give a few elements their shape, and to hold their structure.

Hooks: the following hooks are used in the projects.

UK	US
4mm	G/6
4.5mm	7
5mm	H/8
5.5mm	I/9
6mm	J/10
7mm	K/10½
8mm	L/11

Please note there is no direct US hook size conversion from 7mm, but we have suggested the nearest lower size (US K/10½). However you should adjust your hook size as necessary to achieve an even gauge.

Stitch markers: You will need a removable stitch marker for when you are working in spirals, to keep track of where each "round" of the spiral starts and ends. The pattern will tell you where to place the marker (pm) and it should be moved up as you complete each round. They come in all shapes and sizes, just ensure it is removable!

Tape measure: Always handy for making sure your finished outfit will fit the recipient.

Tapestry needle: A blunt ended needle with a large eye for sewing up and weaving in ends.

Yarn: There are two main thicknesses of yarn used in the projects, DK (Light Worsted) weight and Chunky weight. Please use the following yardage information as a guide when selecting your yarn:
DK (Light Worsted) weight: 328yds (300m) per 3½oz (100g)
Chunky weight: 153yds (140m) per 3½oz (100g)
  You will also find additional specialty yarns featuring in a few of the projects, including the Mermaid and Unicorn. Details for these are given with each project.
  The phrase "small quantity" is used for projects or features that tend to use less than 25g (1oz) of yarn. In some case you will only need a very small amount of a particular colour.

PATTERN NOTES

Each costume has the yarn, hooks, and notions listed for each individual item, making it easy to mix and match different pieces from the various outfits. If you are making the full costume, please ensure you check how much yarn and what equipment you will need to complete it before you start.

SKILL LEVEL

Each project includes a star rating as a skill level guide and you will find the project includes the techniques listed below:

★ Projects for first-time crocheters, using basic stitches, with minimal shaping.

★★ Projects using basic stitches, repetitive stitch patterns, simple colour changes, and simple shaping and finishing.

★★★ Projects using a variety of techniques, such as basic lace patterns or colour patterns, mid-level shaping, and finishing.

The Costumes

In the following pages you'll find full instructions for crocheting and making up the different elements of the costumes, plus helpful tips, and suggestions for what else to wear to complete the look.

Pete the Pirate

A short drive from where we live is a coastal town that has an annual "Pirate Day" to see if they can break the world record for the number of people dressed as a pirate. I'd only just learned to crochet when we decided to head over in all our pirate finery to be part of the event. I looked around everywhere for a little crocheted skull and crossbones to sew onto my youngest son's outfit, but couldn't find quite the right one. The skull and crossbones is the first appliqué pattern I ever made and has since been used numerous times, for everything from babygrows to bunting. The next year a hat, beard, and eye patch followed, and then after some pleading from my eldest son, the parrot popped up to finish it off. This costume hasn't just been used for "Pirate Day" – we regularly dig it out for wearing to school on fancy dress days, or just at home when we're playing pirates on our bed-ship.

Complete the Look

You can get really carried away with this one and go for a full pirate-style white shirt, wasitcoat, breeches and stripy socks, or keep it simple with a striped t-shirt, and a rolled-up pair of pants. The beard pattern could be used as part of a Viking outfit, or how about a bearded lady circus costume!

Beard

SKILL LEVEL ✶✶   A pirate needs a beard – just imagine trying to shave with a cut-throat razor on the high seas!

You will need

Yarn

DK (Light Worsted) weight:
25g (1oz) of Brown (or your colour of choice)

Hooks & Notions

5mm (US 8/H) crochet hook
Tapestry needle

Tension

Tension is not critical but the fabric should be firm yet flexible.

Size

One size: To fit 4-7 years
16.5cm (6½in) wide x 10cm (4in) long (including moustache)

Abbreviations

See page 8.

Pattern Notes

You can easily adapt the beard to fit smaller or larger children by making the loops over the ears shorter or longer.

For the Moustache

Leaving a long tail, make 30ch.
Row 1: Ss in second ch from hook, 1dc in next ch, 1htr in next 2 ch, 1tr in next 2 ch, 1dtr in next 2 ch, 1trtr in next 2 ch, 1dtr in next ch, 1tr in next ch, 1htr in next ch, 1dc in next ch, ss in next ch, 1dc in next ch, 1htr in next ch, 1tr in next ch, 1dtr in next ch, 1trtr in next 2 ch, 1htr in next 2 ch, 1tr in next 2 ch, 1htr in next 2 ch, 1dc in next ch, ss in last ch.
Fasten off, leaving a long tail.

For the Beard

Leaving a long tail, make 23ch.
Row 1: 1tr in fourth ch from hook, 1tr in each st to end, turn. (21 sts)
Row 2: 3ch (counts as 1tr now and throughout), 1tr in next 9 sts, 3tr in next st, 1tr in next 10 sts, turn. (23 sts)
Row 3: 3ch, 1tr in next 19 sts, 1dc in next 3 sts, turn.
Row 4: Dc2tog, 1tr in next 19 sts, dc2tog. (21 sts)
Row 5: 1ch (does not count as a st), tr2tog, 1tr in next 17 sts, tr2tog, 1dc in next st, 1ch, turn. (19 sts)
Row 6: 1ch (does not count as a st), *tr2tog, 1tr in next st; rep from * a further five times, ss in last st to finish. (13 sts)
Fasten off, leaving a long tail.

Finishing

Using the long tails from the beard, sew the corners of the beard to the moustache and tie the long tails on the moustache to make loops to hook over your pirates' ears.

Eye Patch

SKILL LEVEL ✶✶ Every self-respecting pirate wears his scars –
and his eye patch – with pride.

You will need

Yarn
DK (Light Worsted) weight:
Small quantity of Black

Hooks & Notions
4mm (US G/6) crochet hook
Tapestry needle

Tension
Tension is not critical but adjust
the hook size to produce a
firm fabric.

Size
One size:
Patch: 5.5 x 3cm (2¼ x 1¼in)
Ties: Adjust to fit

Abbreviations
See page 8.

For the Patch

Row 1: Make a magic ring and ss to
secure. Work 1ch, 5dc into ring.
Keeping the sts as a semicircle, pull
the starting tail tight, turn. (5 sts)
Row 2: 3ch, 1tr in base of ch, 2tr in
each st to end, turn. (10 sts)
Row 3: 3ch, 1tr in base of ch, 1tr in
next st, *2tr in next st, 1tr in next st;
rep from * a further 3 times. (15 sts)
Row 4 (ties): Make 90ch (or length
required).
Fasten off.
Rejoin yarn at opposite end of
the patch, make 90ch (or
to match the first tie),
Fasten off.

Finishing

Weave in ends. Use the chain ties to
secure the patch around your little
pirate's head.

Tricorn Hat

This traditional hat tops off the outfit. Add the skull and crossbones motif (page 19) to scare your enemies!

You will need

Yarn

Chunky weight:
75g (2¾oz) of Black

4ply (Fingering) weight:
Small amount of Gold metallic for edging

Note: If you can't find a metallic yarn, substitute it with an alternative 4ply (Fingering) weight yarn in a contrast colour.

Hooks & Notions

8mm (US L/11) crochet hook
Tapestry needle

Tension

Tension is not critical but adjust the hook size to produce a firm fabric.

Size

One size: To fit 4-7 years
56cm (22in) circumference

Abbreviations

See page 8.

Pattern Notes

To make a smaller hat, omit Row 7.

To make a bigger hat, work an additional row after Row 7, working an extra 1tr every sixth stitch to give you 48 sts at the end.

For the Hat

Round 1: Make a magic ring and ss to secure. Work 6dc into ring, ss in first dc to join. (6 sts)

Round 2: 3ch, 1tr in base of ch, 2tr in each st to end, ss in third ch of t-ch to join. (12 sts)

Round 3: 3ch, 1tr in base of ch, 1tr in next st, *2tr in next st, 1tr in next st; rep from * a further four times, ss in third ch of t-ch to join. (18 sts)

Round 4: 3ch, 1tr in base of ch, 1tr in next 2 sts, *2tr in next st, 1tr in next 2 sts; rep from * a further four times, ss in third ch of t-ch to join. (24 sts)

Round 5: 3ch, 1tr in base of ch, 1tr in next 3 sts, *2tr in next st, 1tr in next 3 sts; rep from * a further four times, ss in third ch of t-ch to join. (30 sts)

Round 6: 3ch, 1tr in base of ch, 1tr in next 4 sts, *2tr in next st, 1tr in next 4 sts; rep from * a further four times, ss in third ch of t-ch to join. (36 sts)

Round 7: 3ch, 1ch in base of ch, 1tr in next 5 sts, *2tr in next st, 1tr in next 5 sts; rep from * a further four times, ss in third ch of t-ch to join. (42 sts)

Rounds 8-12: 3ch, 1tr in each st to end, ss in third ch of t-ch to join.

Do not fasten off and continue for the Brim as follows:

Round 13: 3ch, 1tr in base of ch, 1tr in next 4 sts, *2tr in next st, 1tr in next 4 sts; rep from * a further six times, 2tr in next st, 1tr in last st, ss in third ch of t-ch to join. (51 sts)

Round 14: 3ch, 1tr in base of ch, 1tr in next 4 sts, *2tr in next st, 1tr in next 4 sts; rep from * a further eight times, 2tr in last st, ss in third ch of t-ch to join. (62 sts)

Round 15: 3ch, *2tr in next st, 1tr in next 4 sts; rep from * a further eleven times, 2dc in last st, ss in third ch of t-ch to join. (75 sts)

Round 16: 3ch, *2tr in next st, 1tr in next 4 sts; rep from * a further thirteen times, 2dc in next st, 1dc in next 3 sts, ss in third ch of t-ch to join. (90 sts)

Round 17: 3ch, 1tr in each st to end, ss in third ch of t-ch to join. Make three, short flat sections in your circle for the "corners" as follows:

Round 18: 3ch, 1tr in each of next 21 sts, 1dc in next st, ss in next 5 sts, 1dc in next st; *1tr in each of next 22 sts, 1dc in next st, ss in next 5 sts, 1dc in next st; rep from * once more, 1dc in last st. Fasten off.

Weave in all loose ends.

Finishing

Join gold metallic thread at any edge stitch, work 1ch, 1dc in each st around, ss in first dc to join. Fasten off. Shape the hat as follows:

Find the centre of each flattened section (the middle slip stitch of the five slip stitches worked in Round 18). Fold them together, lifting the brim up around the body of the hat to form the three corners of your Tricorn Hat. Take a short length of yarn and using the tapestry needle, put a few stitches through each corner to keep each side together. Using a little more yarn, sew a few more stitches through the lifted brim to the body of the hat to keep it up and ensure it keeps its shape.

Skull & Crossbones Motif

SKILL LEVEL ✶ ✶   This skull and crossbones can be made in a larger size (see Pattern Notes, below) to adorn a flag, or to pin on a jacket.

You will need

Yarn

DK (Light Worsted) weight:
Small quantity of White

Hooks & Notions

4mm (US G/6) crochet hook
Tapestry needle

Tension

Tension is not critical but adjust the hook size to produce a firm fabric.

Size

One size:
Skull: 4 x 5cm (1½ x 2in)
Crossbones: 4 x 2.5cm (1½ x 1in)

Abbreviations

See page 8.

Pattern Notes

Make this motif in smaller or larger sizes by simply changing the thickness of the yarn and using a hook size suited to it. It is perfect for using up oddments of yarn from your stash.

For the Skull

Row 1: 8ch, 1tr in fourth ch from hook, 1tr in next 4 sts, turn. (5 sts)
Row 2: 3ch, 1tr in each st to end.
These are the teeth.
Continue as follows to form the eye sockets:
Row 3: 8ch, miss 1 st, 1dc in next st, 8ch, ss in last st, turn.
Continue as follows to complete the skull:
Row 4: 3ch, [2tr, 2dtr, 3trtr] around 8ch-sp, 1trtr in dc, [3trtr, 2dtr, 3tr] in next 8ch-sp.
Fasten off.

For the Crossbones (make 2)

Make 13ch, ss in fourth ch from hook, 3ch, ss in same ch as before, ss down the chain, 3ch, ss in end of original chain, 3ch, ss in same ch as before. Fasten off.

Finishing

Join bones together in the middle, then attach them with a couple of stitches at the bottom corners of the skull. Stitch in place on the tricorn hat or wherever you like!

Parrot

SKILL LEVEL ✶✶   Polly Parrot knows where the "pieces of eight" are buried – but will she tell you?

You will need

Yarn
DK (Light Worsted) weight:
25g (1oz) of (**A**) Red
Small quantities of (**B**) White, and
(**C**) Yellow

Hooks & Notions
5.5mm (US I/9) crochet hook
Small amount of toy stuffing
Two 0.5cm (¼in) black beads plus
needle and thread to match
Removable stitch marker
Tapestry needle

Tension
Tension is not critical but adjust the
hook size to produce a firm fabric.

Size
One size:
14cm (5½in) tall (excluding feet)

Abbreviations
See page 8.

For the Head

Round 1: Using A, make a magic ring and ss to secure. Work 5dc into ring, ss in first dc to join. (5 sts)
Round 2: 1ch, 2dc in each st, ss in first dc to join. (10 sts)
Round 3: 1ch, *2dc in next st, 1dc in next st; rep from * a further four times. (15 sts)
Round 4: 1ch, *2dc in next st, 1dc in next 2 sts; rep from * a further four times. (20 sts)
Rounds 5-9: 1ch, 1dc in each st to end.
Round 10: *Dc2tog, 1dc in next 2 sts; rep from * a further four times, ss in first dc to join. (15 sts)
Round 11: *Dc2tog, 1dc in next st; rep from * a further four times, ss in first dc to join. (10 sts)
Stuff the head and continue as follows:
Round 12: [Dc2tog] five times. (5 sts)
Round 13: [Dc2tog] twice, 1dc, ss in first dc to join.
Fasten off, leaving a long tail for sewing the head to the body.

For the Eyes (make 2)

Using B, make a magic ring and ss to secure. Work 6dc into ring, ss in first dc to join. Fasten off.
Use the tails to sew the eyes to either side of the head.

For the Beak

Using C, make 4ch.
Row 1: 1dc in second ch from hook, 1dc in next 2 ch, turn. (3 sts)
Row 2: 1ch, 1dc in next 2 sts, turn. (2 sts)

Row 3: 1ch, 1dc in next st.
Fasten off, leaving a long tail. Use the tail to sew the beak to the head. Weave in loose ends.

For the Body

Round 1: Using A, make 12ch, ss in first ch to join taking care not to twist the sts.

Rounds 2-3: 1ch, 1dc in each ch, ss in first dc to join. (12 sts)

Round 4: 1ch, *1dc in next 3 sts, 2dc in next st; rep from * twice more, ss in first dc to join. (15 sts)

Round 5: 1ch, 1dc in each st around, ss in first dc to join.

Round 6: 1ch, *1dc in next 4 sts, 2dc in next st; rep from * twice more, ss in first dc to join. (18 sts)

Round 7: 1ch, 1dc in each st around, ss in first dc to join.

Round 8: 1ch, *1dc in next 5 sts, 2dc in next st; rep from * twice more, ss in first dc to join. (21 sts)

Round 9: 1ch, 1dc in each st around, ss in first dc to join.

Round 10: 1ch, *1dc in next 6 sts, 2dc in next st; rep from * twice more, ss in first dc to join. (24 sts)

Round 11: 1ch, *1dc in next 7 sts, 2dc in next st; rep from * twice more, ss in first dc to join. (27 sts)

Round 12: 1ch, *1dc in next 3 sts, dc2tog; rep from * a further four times, 1dc in last 2 sts, ss in first dc to join. (22 sts)

Round 13: 1ch, *1dc in next 2 sts, dc2tog; rep from * a further four times, 1dc in last 2 sts, ss in first dc to join. (17 sts)

Round 14: 1ch, *1dc in next st, dc2tog; rep from * a further four times, 1dc in last 2 sts, ss in first dc to join. (12 sts)
Stuff the body and continue as follows:

Round 15: [Dc2tog] six times, ss in first dc to join. (6 sts)

Round 16: [Dc2tog] three times, ss in first dc to join.
Fasten off.
Securely attach the head to the open end of the body.

For the Tail

Using A, make 8ch.

Row 1: 1dc in second ch from hook, 1dc in each st to end, turn. (7 sts)

Row 2: 1ch, 1dc in each st across, turn.

Rows 3-5: 3ch, 1tr in each st across, turn.

Row 6: *4ch, 1trtr in next st, 4ch, ss in next st; rep from * twice more. Fasten off. This creates the three feathers.

Row 7: Join C in fourth ch of t-ch on Row 6. Work 3ch, 1trtr in next st, 3ch, ss in top of last st in current feather. Fasten off. Repeat for remaining feathers.

For the Wings (make 2)

Using A, make 9ch.

Row 1: 1dc in second ch from hook, 1dc in next 6 ch, 3dc in last ch. (10 sts)

Row 2: Working up the other side of foundation ch, 1dc in next 7 sts, 2dc in end ch, ss in first dc of Row 1 to join. (19 sts)
Work in rounds as follows:

Round 1: 1ch, 1dc in next 9 sts, [1dc, 1tr, 1dc] in next st, 1dc in the next 9 sts, ss in first dc to join. (21 sts)

Round 2: 1ch, 2dc in next st, 1dc in next 9 sts, [1dc, 1tr, 1dc] in next st, 1dc in next 10 sts, ss in first dc to join. (22 sts)
Fasten off.

Finishing

Attach tail and wings to the body and weave in all ends.
Pop the beads in the middle of the eye circles securing with the needle and thread, then with a whistle and a "pretty Polly" your parrot is all finished!

Little Mermaid

This was a costume inspired by a little girl who LOVES dressing up and was desperate to be a mermaid. She had played with some of the other dress-up crochet and her mum approached me the next day and said: "You know, Ava would be thrilled if you could make a mermaid costume." Well, I only usually have boys to make things for, so I grabbed the chance to make something girly. The tail pays homage to granny chic and the classic granny square, which is the first thing I ever learned to crochet. The mermaid hair is still one of my favourite makes ever, in fact I made it just big enough for me to wear.

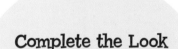

Complete the Look

Turquoise leggings and a peppermint coloured vest top are ideal for this, but a swimming costume works perfectly, too.

Hair

SKILL LEVEL ✶ ✶ These long locks in seaweed colors will make your mermaid look as if she has just stepped out of the sea.

Pattern Notes

For a smaller size, omit Rounds 3, 5 and the two sets of 5 ss.

You will need

Yarn

Chunky weight:
100g (3½oz) each of (**A**) Teal, (**B**) Mint, and (**C**) Turquoise

Metallic 4ply (Fingering) weight: 25g (1oz) of (**D**) Dark green

Note: If you can't find a metallic yarn, substitute it with an alternative 4ply (Fingering) weight yarn in a suitable colour.

Hooks & Notions

8mm (US L/11) crochet hook
Tapestry needle

Tension

Tension is not critical but the fabric should be firm yet flexible.

Size

One size: To fit 4-7 years
51cm (20in) circumference

Abbreviations

See page 8.

For the Hair

Round 1: Using A, B, C, and D held together as one strand, make a magic ring and secure with ss. Work 6dc into ring, ss in first dc to join. (6 sts)

Round 2: 3ch (counts as 1tr now and throughout), 1tr in base of ch, 2tr in each st around, ss in third ch of t-ch to join. (12 sts)

Round 3: 3ch, 1tr in base of ch, 1tr in next st, *2tr in next st, 1tr in next st; rep from * a further four times, ss in third ch of t-ch to join. (18 sts)

Round 4: 3ch, 1tr in base of ch, 1tr in next 2 sts, *2tr in next st, 1tr in next 2 sts; rep from * a further four times, ss in third ch of t-ch to join. (24 sts)

Round 5: 3ch, 1tr in base of ch, 1tr in next 3 sts, *2tr in next st, 1tr in next 3 sts; rep from * a further four times, ss in third ch of t-ch to join. (30 sts)

Rounds 6–7: 1ch, 1dc in each st around, ss in first dc to join.

Do not fasten off and continue as follows to create the hair:

Steps 1–9: *Make 51ch, 1dc in second ch from hook, 1dc in each ch, 1dc in next st of hat brim to secure; rep from * a further nine times.

Step 10: Ss in next 5 sts along the edge of the hat.

Steps 11–19: *Make 41ch, 1dc in second ch from hook, 1dc in each ch, 1dc in next st of hat brim to secure; rep from * a further nine times.

Step 20: Ss in next 5 sts along the edge of the hat.

Fasten off.

Finishing

Create a centre parting along the top of the hair as follows:
Take the 10 longer strands and part them in the middle. Bring the fifth one on each side around to the back, ensuring that the four remaining strands of the bundle are held underneath them, and secure together at the side and back of the hat with a few stitches.

Tail

SKILL LEVEL ★ ★   Pick as many colours from the ocean as you like to make the mermaid's tail – it's perfect for using up oddments from your stash.

You will need

Yarn
Chunky weight:
100g (3½oz) each of (**A**) Teal, (**B**) Mint, and (**C**) Turquoise

Hooks & Notions
7mm (US K/10½) crochet hook

Co-ordinating ribbon—2cm (¾in) wide x 203cm (80in) long

Tapestry needle

Tension
Tension is not critical but the fabric should be firm yet flexible.

Size
One size: To fit ages 4-7
51cm (20in) circumference

Abbreviations
See page 8.

For the Tail

Row 1: Using C, make 53ch, 1tr in fourth ch from hook, 1tr in each st to end, turn. (51 sts)

Rows 2-6: 3ch (counts as 1tr now and throughout), 1tr in each st across, turn. Fasten off C.

Row 7: Join B, 3ch, 2tr in same st, *1ch, miss 2 sts, 3tr in next st; rep from * a further 16 times, 3ch, ss in third ch of t-ch in Row 6. Fasten off B. (17 granny sts)

Row 8: Join A in top of last tr of previous row, turn. 3ch, *3tr in ch-sp, 1ch; rep from * a further fifteen times, 3ch, ss in third ch of t-ch in row below. Fasten off A. (16 granny sts)

Row 9: Join C in top of last tr of previous row, turn. 3ch, *3tr in ch-sp, 1ch; rep from * a further fourteen times, 3ch, ss in third ch of t-ch in row below. Fasten off C. (15 granny sts)

Row 10: Join B in top of last tr of previous row, turn. 3ch, *3tr in ch-sp, 1ch; rep from * a further thirteen times, 3ch, ss in third ch of t-ch in row below. Fasten off B. (14 granny sts)

Row 11: Join A in top of last tr of previous row, turn. 3ch, *3tr in ch-sp, 1ch; rep from * a further twelve times, 3ch, ss in third ch of t-ch in row below. (13 granny sts)

Row 12: Join C in top of last tr of previous row, turn. 3ch, *3tr in ch-sp, 1ch; rep from * a further eleven times, 3ch, ss in third ch of t-ch in row below. (12 granny sts)

Row 13: Join B in top of last tr of previous row, turn. 3ch, *3tr in ch-sp, 1ch; rep from * a further ten times, 3ch, ss in third ch of t-ch in row below. (11 granny sts)

Row 14: Join A in top of last tr of previous row, turn. 3ch, *3tr in ch-sp, 1ch; rep from * a further nine times, 3ch, ss in third ch of t-ch in row below. (10 granny sts)

Row 15: Join C in top of last tr of previous row, turn. 3ch, *3tr in ch-sp, 1ch; rep from * a further eight times, 3ch, ss in third ch of t-ch in row below. (9 granny sts)

Row 16: Join B in top of last tr of previous row, turn. 3ch, *3tr in ch-sp, 1ch; rep from *a further seven times, 3ch, ss in third ch of t-ch in row below. (8 granny sts)

Pattern Notes

The tail is designed to be knee length, allowing for proper running around, and because you can adjust the width with the ribbons it will fit pretty much anyone.

This pattern uses a good old-fashioned granny square stitch made-up of 3 treble stitches worked into a chain space. You use the number of granny square stitches to keep track of where you are throughout the pattern.

Row 17: Join A in top of last tr of previous row, turn. 3ch, *3tr in ch-sp, 1ch; rep from * a further six times, 3ch, ss in third ch of t-ch in row below. (7 granny sts)

Row 18: Join C in top of last tr of previous row, turn. 3ch, *3tr in ch-sp, 1ch; rep from * a further five times, 3ch, ss in third ch of t-ch in row below. (6 granny sts)

Row 19: Join B in top of last tr of previous row, turn. 3ch, *3tr in ch-sp, 1ch; rep from * a further four times, 3ch, ss in third ch of t-ch in row below. (5 granny sts)

Row 20: Join A in top of last tr of previous row, turn. 3ch, *3tr in ch-sp, 1ch; rep from * a further three times, 3ch, ss in third ch of t-ch in row below. (4 granny sts)

Row 21: Join C in top of last tr of previous row, turn. 3ch, *3tr in ch-sp, 1ch; rep from * twice more, 3ch, ss in third ch of t-ch in row below. (3 granny sts)

Row 22: Join B in top of last tr of previous row, turn. 3ch, *3tr in ch-sp, 1ch; rep from * once more, 3ch, ss in third ch of t-ch in row below. (2 granny sts)

Row 23: Join A in top of last tr of previous row, 3ch, 3tr in ch-sp, 3ch, ss in corner st of previous row to finish.

Fins (make 2)

Round 1: Using C, make 16ch, 1dc in second ch from hook, *1dc in next ch, 1htr in next 2 ch, 1tr in next 2 ch, 1dtr in next ch, 1trtr in next ch, 1dtr in next ch,

1tr in next 2 ch, 1htr in next 2 ch, 1dc in next ch, 1dc in last ch; working down opposite side of the chain, 1dc in first ch; rep from * once more.

Round 2: Working around the previous row, 2dc in first st, *1dc in next 7 sts, 2dc in next st; rep from * twice more, 1dc in next 6 sts. Fasten off.
Work the edging as follows:

Round 3: Join B, work *2ch, ss in next st; rep from * to end.
Fasten off.

Finishing

Attach the fins either side of the final granny stitch of the mermaid tail.
Weave in all ends and block gently according to the ball band.
Take the ribbon and weave it in and out of the top row of treble crochet stitches of the tail, leaving a good even length at each side. Thread each length across the edges (as though lacing your shoes) and attach to your little mermaid.

Little Crab

SKILL LEVEL ✶ ✶ This cute little crab completes the mermaid's outfit – you can pin it to the tail, or leave it loose to be carried.

You will need

Yarn

DK (Light Worsted) weight:
Small quantity of Red

Hooks & Notions

4mm (US G/6) crochet hook
Small amount of toy stuffing
Two black beads
Black embroidery thread
Needle and black sewing thread
Tapestry needle

Tension

Tension is not critical but adjust the hook size to produce a firm fabric.

Size

One size: 2.5cm (1in) across (excluding claws)

Abbreviations

See page 8.

Pattern Notes

The legs and claws are made separately then sewn into the body of the crab later, so when you fasten off, leave long tails for stitching with.

For the Body

Round 1: Make a magic ring and secure with ss. Work 4dc into ring, ss in first dc to join. (4 sts)
Round 2: 1ch, 2dc in each st around, ss in first dc to join. (8 sts)
Round 3: 1ch, *2dc in next st, 1dc in next st; rep from * a further three times, ss in first dc to join. (12 sts)
Round 4: 1ch, 1dc in each st around, ss in first dc to join.
Round 5: [Dc2tog] six times, ss in first dc to join. (6 sts)
Stuff the body.
Round 6: [Dc2tog] three times, ss in first dc to join. (3 sts)
Fasten off and use the tail to close the small opening.

For the Legs (make 6)

Make 6ch.
Fasten off, leaving a long tail.

For the Claws (make 2)

Make 8ch, 1dc in fifth ch from hook, 1ch, ss to finish.
Fasten off, leaving a long tail.

Finishing

Using the long tails, stitch the legs and claws onto the body. Weave the ends in through the legs and into the body, pulling them tightly to give them their shape.
Securely stitch the beads on for eyes and add a few stitches for the mouth.

Superhero

Having two boys of my own, and four nephews, all between the ages of two and eight years, there's a lot of superhero play that goes on. The hero mask was one of the first real costume pieces that I ever made, and very quickly there were requests from all the little boys in my life. This really is the single most worn costume in our house, partly because my youngest wore it every day for a whole summer, but also because the mask doubles up as a winter hat. The good thing is, because it's made of yarn they can fall asleep wearing it in the back of the car, and it isn't uncomfortable. This is a great basic pattern you can embellish in a hundred different ways to create a whole gang of crime-fighting superheroes, or add Lucha Libra-style decoration, and the pattern doubles up as a wrestling outfit!

Complete the Look

Pyjamas are perfect for this, or use a t-shirt and tracksuit bottoms. Underpants over the top are optional!

Mask

This mask does double duty as a hat – useful when my youngest refuses to wear one, which is most days!

You will need

Yarn
Chunky weight:
50g (2oz) of (**A**) Electric blue
DK (Light Worsted) weight:
Small quantity of (**B**) White

Hooks & Notions
4mm (US G/6) crochet hook
5.5mm (US I/9) crochet hook
Tapestry needle

Tension
Tension is not critical but adjust the hook size to produce a firm fabric.

Size
One size: To fit 4-7 years
47cm (18½in) circumference

Abbreviations
See page 8.

For the Mask

Round 1: Using A and 5.5mm (US I/9) hook, make a magic ring and secure with ss. 3ch (counts as 1tr now and throughout), work 11tr into ring, ss in third ch of t-ch to join. (12 sts)

Round 2: 3ch, 1tr in base of ch, 2tr in each st around, ss in third ch of t-ch to join. (24 sts)

Round 3: 3ch, 1tr in base of ch, 1tr in next st, *2tr in next st, 1tr in next st; rep from * to end, ss in third ch of t-ch to join. (36 sts)

Round 4: 3ch, 1tr in base of ch, 1tr in next 2 sts, *2tr in next st, 1tr in next 2 sts; rep from * to end, ss in third ch of t-ch to join. (48 sts)

Rounds 5-12: 3ch, 1tr in each st around, ss in third ch of t-ch to join.

Round 13: 3ch, 1tr in next 10 sts, 1dtr in next st, 1trtr in next st, 10ch, miss 6 sts, 1trtr in next 2 sts, 10ch, miss 6 sts, 1trtr in next st, 1dtr in next st, 1tr in each st to end. (36 sts and two 10ch-sp eyeholes)

Round 14: 3ch, 1tr in each st to eyeholes, 8tr around the whole chain (rather than through the sts), 1tr in each st between the eyes, 8tr around second eyehole chain, 1tr in each of next 5 sts, tr2tog, 1tr in next 5 sts, tr2tog, 1tr in next 5 sts, tr2tog, ss in third ch of t-ch to join.

Fasten off.

Pattern Notes

Adjust the size to fit 2-3 years by omitting Round 4.

To make the hat a little bit stretchier, use a US K/10½ (7mm) crochet hook and omit Round 4.

For the Star Motif

Using B and 4mm (US G/6) hook, make 3ch, ss in first ch to make a ring.
Round 1: 1ch, 10dc into the ring. (10 sts)
Round 2: *5ch, ss in second ch from hook, 1dc in next ch, 1htr in next ch, 1tr in last ch, miss 1 st, ss in next st; rep from * a further 4 times.
Fasten off, leaving a long tail.

Finishing

Use the long tail of the star motif to stitch it to the mask at the centre front between the eyeholes. Weave in all loose ends.

Cuffs

SKILL LEVEL ✶ ✶

When you're wrestling with evil, you need to protect yourself. These superhero cuffs will do the job.

You will need

Yarn
Chunky weight:
38g (1½oz) of (**A**) Electric Blue

DK (Light Worsted) weight:
Small quantity of (**B**) White

Hooks & Notions
5.5mm (US I/9) crochet hook
Tapestry needle

Tension
Tension is not critical but adjust the hook size to produce a firm fabric.

Size
One size: To fit 4-7 years –
see pattern notes
Length: 13.5cm (5¼in)
Circumference: 15cm (6in)

Abbreviations
See page 8.

For the Cuffs (make 2)
Using yarn A, make 18ch.
Row 1: 1tr in fourth ch from hook, 1tr in each ch to end, turn. (16 sts)
Rows 2-12: 3ch (counts as 1tr now and throughout), working into the back loop only 1tr in each st to end, turn.
Fasten off, leaving a long tail.

For the Fins (make 6)
Using A, make 5ch, ss in second ch from hook, 1dc in next st, 1htr in next st, 3tr in next st.
Fasten off, leaving a long tail.

For the Star Motif (make 2)
Follow the instructions for the Star Motif on page 33.

Finishing
Using the long tails, attach three fins in a line down the centre of each cuff, then stitch the star motif in place. Sew the long edges together.
  Weave in all loose ends.

Pattern Notes
Create superhero forearm shields by making a longer starting chain.

Make these for younger or older children by working fewer or more repeats of the double crochet row.

Chest Plate

SKILL LEVEL ★ ★   Every hero needs to have his own symbol on his chest, to be instantly recognised by enemies and grateful humans alike.

You will need

Yarn
Chunky weight:
75g (2¾oz) of (**A**) Electric Blue
DK (Light Worsted) weight:
Small quantity of (**B**) White

Hooks & Notions
4mm (US G/6) crochet hook
5.5mm (US I/9) crochet hook
Tapestry needle

Tension
Tension is not critical but adjust the hook size to produce a firm fabric.

Size
One size: To fit 4-7 years – see pattern notes on page 35
Chest: 66cm (26in) circumference

Abbreviations
See page 8.

For the Chest Plate
Using A and 5.5mm
(US I/9) hook, make
81ch.
Row 1: 1dc in second ch from hook, 1dc in each st to end, turn. (80 sts)
Rows 2-11: 1ch, 1dc in each st across, turn.
Fasten off, leaving a long tail.

For the Straps (make 2)
Using A and 5.5mm (US I/9) hook, make 7ch.
Row 1: 1dc in second ch from hook, 1dc in each st to the end, turn. (6 sts)
Row 2: 1ch, 1dc in each st across, turn.
Fasten off, leaving a long tail.

For the Star Motif (make 1)
Follow the instructions for the Star Motif on page 33.

Finishing
Sew the short sides of the plate together. Lie the chest plate flat, with the centre seam facing you. Attach each strap to the chest plate approximately 8 sts from the centre seam. Miss 14 sts and attach the other end of the strap to chest plate.
Stitch the star motif to the centre front of the chest plate.
Weave in all loose ends.

Snow Queen

We were snowed in a couple of winters ago and my boys and I started looking for winter stories to read. *The Snow Queen* by Hans Christian Andersen was one of my favourites as a child, so I dug out my old book of fairy tales and we read it together. My eldest asked if we could "play" Snow Queen and this outfit is what popped into my head.

This is the first time I ever thought to crochet using two yarns together, as I knew I needed the sturdiness of a regular yarn but really wanted something sparkly too. As I couldn't find a suitable single yarn, I bought two – one sparkly and one regular, then crocheted holding them together as one strand. The result had just the right level of "cold and icy" that I'd been looking for.

Complete the Look

This pattern caught the eye of our neighbours' daughter who trotted over in a very pretty, white lace bridesmaid's dress, put all these on, and went off to play in the park. You may not have a spare bridesmaid's dress lying around, but a simple white or pale blue cotton dress makes a perfect Snow Queen gown.

Snowflake Crown

SKILL LEVEL ★★   A crown made from snowflakes is perfect for the queen of winter.

You will need

Yarn

DK (Light Worsted) weight:
Small quantity of White

Metallic 4ply (Fingering) weight:
Small quantity of White or Silver

Note: If you can't find a metallic yarn, substitute it with an alternative 4ply (Fingering) weight yarn in a suitable colour.

Hooks & Notions

4.5mm (US 7) crochet hook
Tapestry needle

Tension

Tension is not critical but adjust the hook size to produce a firm fabric.

Size

One size: To fit 4-7 years
46cm (18in) circumference

Abbreviations

See page 8.

Pattern Notes

All elements for the Snow Queen outfit are worked holding the two yarns (white and metallic) together throughout. If preferred, you can find a suitable sparkly yarn and use that instead.

For the Snowflake Motif (make 3)

Make 5ch, ss in first ch to join in a ring.

Round 1: 3ch, working into centre of ring make 1tr, *3ch, 2tr; rep from * a further three times, ss in third ch of t-ch to join.

Round 2: 1ch, 1dc in third ch of t-ch, *[1dc, 5ch, 1dc] in 3ch-sp, miss 1 tr, 1dc in next st; rep from * a further four times, ss in first dc to join.

Round 3: *3ch, [ss, 5ch, ss, 3ch, sl st] in 5ch-sp, ss in next st, ss in centre dc**, ss in 5ch-sp; rep from * a further four times, ending last repeat at **.
Fasten off, leaving a long tail.

For the Band

Leaving a long tail, make 37ch. Work 1tr in fourth ch from hook, 1tr in each ch to the end. Fasten off, leaving a long tail.

Finishing

Lay the snowflakes side-by-side with two points at the bottom and one at the top – like a star – and stitch the two bottom points touching one another together using the long tails. Stitch each end of the band to each end of the row of snowflakes.
Weave in all loose ends and block gently according to the ball band.

Snowflake Collar

SKILL LEVEL ✶ ✶ This snowflake collar is so pretty you could wear it over any old jumper, and it would make it look magical.

You will need

Yarn

DK (Light Worsted) weight:
Small quantity of White

Metallic 4ply (Fingering) weight:
Small quantity of White or Silver

Note: If you can't find a metallic yarn, substitute it with an alternative 4ply (Fingering) weight yarn in a suitable colour.

Hooks & Notions

4.5mm (US 7) crochet hook
90cm (36in) white ribbon
Tapestry needle

Tension

Tension is not critical but adjust the hook size to produce a firm fabric.

Size

One size: 32cm (12½in) long (excluding ribbon)

Abbreviations

See page 8.

For the Snowflake Motif (make 5)

Using the pattern for the Snowflake Motif on page 40, make five snowflakes.

Finishing

Join the motifs together in a row as instructed for the Crown on page 40.
Block gently according to the ball band.
Loop the ribbon through either end of the row of snowflakes and tie with a bow on your Snow Queen.

Pattern Notes

All elements for the Snow Queen outfit are worked holding the two yarns (white and metallic) together throughout. If preferred, you can find a suitable sparkly yarn and use that instead.

Icicle Cuffs

SKILL LEVEL ✶ ✶   These pretty wristbands are tied together with ribbon that is woven through the crochet pieces, like laces.

Pattern Notes

All elements for the Snow Queen outfit are worked holding the two yarns (white and metallic) together throughout. If preferred, you can find a suitable sparkly yarn and use that instead.

You will need

Yarn

DK (Light Worsted) weight: Small quantity of White

Metallic 4ply (Fingering) weight: Small quantity of White or Silver

Note: If you can't find a metallic yarn, substitute it with an alternative 4ply (Fingering) weight yarn in a suitable colour.

Hooks & Notions

4.5mm (US 7) crochet hook
90cm (36in) white ribbon
Tapestry needle

Tension

Tension is not critical but adjust the hook size to produce a firm fabric.

Size

One size: 12cm (4¾in) wide, 12.5cm (5in) deep (excluding finger loop and ribbon)

Abbreviations

See page 8.

For the Cuffs (make 2)

Make 28ch.
Row 1: 1tr in eighth ch from hook, *4ch, miss 3 ch, 1tr in next ch; rep from * to end, turn.
Row 2: 5ch, 1tr in first ch-sp, *4ch, 1tr in next ch-sp; rep from * to end, turn.
Repeat Row 2 twice more.
Fasten off.

For the Snowflake Motif (make 2)

Using the pattern for the Snowflake Motif on page 40, make two snowflakes, leaving a long tail as you fasten off.

Finishing

Stitch a snowflake to the middle of the long edge of the mesh band – attach with the two points opposite the finger loop.
Weave in all loose ends.
Block gently according to ball band.
Cut the ribbon in half and use a length for each cuff. Lace the ribbon through the mesh at either short end of the cuff in criss-crosses (just like shoe laces). Tie them in a bow on your Snow Queen's wrists.

Robin Hood

This is a costume I actually forced on the beasts! I loved the Disney movie version of *Robin Hood* when I was little – Robin was a charming fox and Little John a big ol' daddy bear, and even though I tried to get them to love it too, they still prefer more modern movies. Armed with a shiny new crochet hook and chunky green yarn, I thought I could possibly convert them with a quick costume, and once we put some arrows in the quiver, tied the wrist guards on, and popped a feather in the hat, they were away.

Complete the Look

An oversized green t-shirt and a brown belt are all you need to finish this off, but don't forget your bow and arrows!

Hat

Robin's peaked hat, in leafy green, provides great camouflage among the trees of Sherwood Forest – or your back garden.

You will need

Yarn

Chunky weight:
100g (3½oz) of Forest Green

Hooks & Notions

6mm (US J/10) crochet hook

Removable stitch marker

Tapestry needle

Tension

Tension is not critical but adjust the hook size to produce a firm fabric.

Size

One size: To fit 4-7 years
51cm (20in) circumference (before brim); 56cm (24in) after brim; 23cm (9in) tall (with brim folded)

Abbreviations

See page 8.

Pattern Notes

Adjust the size to fit 2-3 years by omitting Round 8.

To make the hat a little bit stretchier, use a 7mm (US K/10½) crochet hook and omit Round 8.

For the Hat

Round 1: Make a magic ring and secure with ss. 3ch (counts as 1tr now and throughout), work 5tr into ring, ss in third ch of t-ch to join. (6 sts)

Round 2: 2ch, 1tr in base of ch, 2tr in each st around, ss in third ch of t-ch to join. (12 sts)

Round 3: 3ch, 1tr in base of ch, 1tr, *2tr in next st, 1tr; rep from * to end, ss in third ch of t-ch to join. (18 sts)

Round 4: 3ch, 1tr in base of ch, 2tr, *2tr in next st, 2tr; rep from * to end, ss in third ch of t-ch to join. (24 sts)

Round 5: 3ch, 1tr in base of ch, 3tr, *2tr in next st, 3tr; rep from * to end, ss in third ch of t-ch to join. (30 sts)

Round 6: 3ch, 1tr in base of ch, 4tr, *2tr in next st, 4tr; rep from * to end, ss in third ch of t-ch to join. (36 sts)

Round 7: 3ch, 1tr in base of ch, 5tr, *2tr in next st, 5tr; rep from * to end, ss in third ch of t-ch to join. (42 sts)

Round 8: 3ch, 1tr in base of ch, 6tr, *2tr in next st, 6tr; rep from * to end, ss in third ch of t-ch to join. (48 sts)

Rounds 9–13: 3ch, 1tr in each st to end, ss in third ch of t-ch to join.

Round 14: 3ch, 1tr in base of ch, 3tr, *2tr in next st, 3tr; rep from * to end, ss in third ch of t-ch to join. (60 sts)

Round 15: 3ch, 1tr in base of ch, 4tr, *2tr in next st, 4tr; rep from * to end, ss in third ch of t-ch to join. (72 sts)

Round 16: 3ch, 1tr in base of ch, 5tr, *2tr in next st, 5tr; rep from * around, ss in third ch of t-ch to join. (84 sts) Do not break yarn and continue as follows in rows to create the Peak:

For the Peak

Row 1: 3ch, 11tr, turn. (12 sts)
Row 2: 1ch, miss 1 st, 1dc in next st, 8tr, 1dc in next st, miss 1 st, ss in next st. (10 sts)
Fasten off.

Finishing

Weave in all ends. Using the tapestry needle threaded with a length of yarn, turn up the brim either side of the peak and secure it in the body of the hat with a few stitches.

Arrow Quiver

SKILL LEVEL ✱ ✱ Robin and his band of outlaws need their arrows ready to hand, for when the Sheriff of Nottingham approaches.

You will need

Yarn
Chunky weight:
50g (1¾oz) of (**A**) Brown
Small quantity of (**B**) White

Hooks & Notions
7mm (US K/10½) crochet hook
Removable stitch marker
Tapestry needle

Tension
Tension is not critical but adjust the hook size to produce a firm fabric.

Size
One size:
Quiver: 24cm (9½in) tall x
10cm (4in) diameter
Strap: 42cm (16½in)
circumference – adjust to fit

Abbreviations
See page 8.

For the Quiver

Round 1: Using A, make a magic ring and secure with ss. Work 1ch, 6dc into ring, ss in first dc to join. (6 sts)

Round 2: 3ch (counts as 1tr now and throughout), 2tr in each st around to marker, ss in third ch of t-ch to join. (12 sts)

Round 3: 3ch, *2tr in next st, 1tr in next st; rep from * around, ss in third ch of t-ch to join. (18 sts)

Round 4: 3ch, *2tr in next st, 1tr in next 2 sts; rep from * around, ss in third ch of t-ch to join. (24 sts)

Round 5: 1ch, working in the back loop only work 1dc in each st around, ss in first dc to join.

Work in spirals (no turning chains required), keeping track of each round with the stitch marker and continue as follows:

Rounds 6-31: 1dc in each st around. Fasten off A.

Round 32: Join B, 1dc in each st around, fasten off B.

Round 33: Rejoin A, 1dc in each st around, ss in first dc to join. Fasten off.

Strap

Using A, make 110ch.

Rows 1-2: 1dc in second ch from hook, 1dc in each ch to end, fasten off A, turn.

Row 3: Join B, 1ch, 1dc in each st around, ss in first dc to join. Fasten off.

Finishing

Using A and the tapestry needle, join the short ends of the strap together and attach to the body of the quiver. Weave in all loose ends.

Wrist Guards

SKILL LEVEL ✱ These wrist guards are super-simple to make, but they really complete the look, and protect the archer's arms!

You will need

Yarn
Chunky weight:
Small quantities of (**A**) Forest Green, and (**B**) Dark Brown

Hooks & Notions
6mm (US J/10) crochet hook
Tapestry needle

Tension
Tension is not critical but the fabric should be firm yet flexible.

Size
One size: To fit 4-7 years
16.5cm (6in) circumference;
12.5cm (4½in) tall

Abbreviations
See page 8.

For the Wrist Guards (make 2)

Using A, make 15ch.
Row 1: 1tr in third ch from hook, 1tr in each st to end, turn. (13 sts)
Rows 2–10: 3ch, 1tr in each st to end, turn.
Fasten off and weave in all ends.

Finishing

Cut twelve 20cm (8in) lengths of B and make ties to attach to the wrist guards as follows:
Fold in half and use the crochet hook to pull the folded end through the fabric, then pass the cut ends through the loop to secure. Secure one at the top, middle, and bottom of either side of the wrist guards and tie the guards around the arms of your Merry Man or Maid Marian.

Forest Fairy

I will confess straight away that neither the flower garland nor the wings were made for anyone other than myself! Every year we go to a celebratory Spring festival where everyone wears flower garlands in their hair. I wanted something pretty, that wouldn't get damaged, and that I could use year after year – crochet seemed the perfect solution. It's so pretty and is comfortable to wear too. The wings followed on from the garland, and are just beautiful! One of the neighbours' daughters came in and begged to wear them, and now they double up as a decoration for my craft room, and dress-up for her.

Complete the Look

A cotton summer dress is all you need to complete this outfit. If your fairy has a favourite dress, you can pick yarn for the flowers in colours to match.

Flower Garland

SKILL LEVEL ✶✶ No need to pick flowers from the forest or garden for this costume, just wear this pretty little garland in your hair.

You will need

Yarn

DK (Light Worsted) weight:
Small quantities of (**A**) Bright Green, (**B**) Dark Green, (**C**) Light Green), (**D**) Yellow, (**E**) Pink, (**F**) Peach, and (**G**) White

Hooks & Notions

4mm (US G/6) crochet hook
Tapestry needle

Tension

Tension is not critical but adjust the hook size to produce a firm fabric.

Size

One size: To fit 4-7 years – see pattern notes
45cm (18in) circumference

Abbreviations

See page 8.

For the Band

Using A and B held together and leaving a long tail, make 70ch.
Work 1dc in second ch from hook, 1dc in each st to end.
Fasten off, leaving a long tail.

For the Flowers

(Make 10 in the following colour combinations—4 using D at the centre and E for the petals, 3 using D at the centre and F for the petals, 3 using G at the centre and D for the petals)
Work as follows:

Round 1: Using centre colour, make 5ch, ss in first ch to join.

Round 2: 1ch, 10dc around the ch. Fasten off centre colour.

Rounds 3-7: Join petal colour, *(1dc, 1tr, 1dc) in next st, ss in next st; rep from * a further four times. Five petals made.

Pattern Notes

The garland can be made to fit anyone, just ensure the starting chain for the band is long enough to go comfortably around their head.

I like to crochet yarns together for a more organic look. All you need to do is hold your yarns together and crochet using them as one strand.

Play with colour and make the flowers and leaves whatever colours you like! Tonal versions would be pretty or go wild using odds and ends from your stash for a Technicolor look.

For the Leaves

Make 50 in the following colours—14 using A, 26 using B, 10 using C. Work as follows:

Make 7ch, 1dc in second ch from hook, 1htr in next st, 1tr in next st, 1dtr in next st, 5tr in next st, working down the opposite side of the chain 1dtr in next 2 sts, 1tr in next st, 1htr in next st, 1dc in next st.

Fasten off, leaving a long tail for sewing together later.

Finishing

Using at least two leaves in B to give the flowers a dark background to stand out against, take five leaves and lay them in a star shape so the tips/edges are all touching and sew them together. Place a flower at the centre and stitch it securely in place. Make a total of ten flower and leaf clusters and attach them to the band. Tie the ends of the band together, weave in all loose ends, and pop it on the head of your fairy.

Corsage

SKILL LEVEL ✶✶   The finishing touch to this forest fairy outfit is a cluster of flowers, to match the garland.

You will need

Yarn
DK (Light Worsted) weight:
Small quantities of (**A**) Bright Green, (**D**) Yellow, (**E**) Pink, (**F**) Peach, and (**G**) White

Hooks & Notions
4mm (US G/6) crochet hook
Tapestry needle

Tension
Tension is not critical but adjust the hook size to produce a firm fabric.

Size
One size: 13cm (5¼in) circumference

Abbreviations
See page 8.

For the Band
Using A, make 25ch.
Row 1: 1dc in second ch from hook, 1dc in each ch to end, turn.
Rows 2-6: 1ch, 1dc in each st to end, turn.
Fasten off.

For the Flowers and Leaves
Using the pattern for the Garland on page 56, make 3 flowers and 1 leaf.

Finishing
Attach leaf to base and then sew the flowers on top of it, sew together the short sides of the base, weave in ends, and then pop this on your fairy's wrist.

Pattern Notes
The corsage is adjustable to fit fairies of all ages! Just ensure the starting chain for the band is long enough to comfortably go around their wrist. This pattern also doubles as a pretty anklet.

Fairy Wings

SKILL LEVEL ★ ★ ★ Make these to be worn, or just to look pretty hanging up in a little girl's (or a grown up's) shabby-chic bedroom.

You will need

Yarn

Small quantities of various yarns including Chunky, Aran, DK (Light Worsted), novelty yarns, and metallic thread held with the main yarn as you work

Hooks & Notions

4mm (US G/6) crochet hook
5.5mm (US I/9) crochet hook
Two wire coat hangers
Wire cutters
Duct tape or similar strong tape
Tapestry needle
2m (2½ yds) white ribbon

Tension

Tension is not critical but adjust the hook size to produce a firm fabric.

Size

One size: To fit 4 years and upward
Each wing is 14 x 38cm (5½ x 15in)

Abbreviations

See page 8.

For the Frame (make 2)

Using the wire cutters, clip the hook off the coat hanger at the shoulder curve. Using duct tape, overlap and bind the ends together to create the frame for the wings. It can be bent and stretched into whatever shape you like.
Using chunky yarn and the larger hook, work double crochet around the frame hooking around the wire to cover it. Fasten off and weave in the loose ends.

For the Motifs

This is where you can get creative and play around creating various motifs to fill the inside of the wing frame. Mix different yarn weights, colours, textures, and motifs for a shabby-chic look, or keep everything uniform by duplicating the same motif – it's entirely up to you!
I used three motifs in each wing: Motifs 1–3 in Wing One and Motifs 2, 3, and 4 in Wing Two.

Motif 1

Make 6ch, ss in first ch to join.
Round 1: 3ch, 11tr in ring. (12 sts)
Round 2: *4ch (counts as 1tr and 1ch), [1tr, 1ch] in each st around, ss in third ch of t-ch to join.
Round 3: 3ch (counts as 1tr), 2tr in base of ch, 3tr in each st around, ss in third ch of t-ch to join.
Round 4: *5ch, miss 2 sts, ss in next st; rep from * a further 11 times.
Round 5: Ss in 5ch-sp, 3ch, 4tr in same ch-sp, 3ch, [5tr, 3ch] in each ch-sp around, ss in third ch of t-ch to join.
Round 6: *5ch, ss in third tr of 5tr in Round 5, 5ch, ss to 3ch-sp, rep from * around. Fasten off.

Motif 2

Make 5ch, ss in first ch to join.

Round 1: 1ch, 10dc in ring. (10 sts)

Round 2: *3ch, miss 1 st, ss in next st; rep from * a further four times.

Round 3: Ss into 3ch-sp, 3ch, 2tr in same ch-sp, 1ch, [3tr, 1ch] in each 3ch-sp around, ss in third ch of t-ch to join. (15 sts and 5 ch-sps)

Round 4: 3ch, and counting the ch-sps as sts, *1tr in next st, 2tr in next st; rep from * around. (30 sts)

Round 5: *5ch, miss 1 st, ss in next st; rep from * around.

Fasten off.

Motif 3

Make 5ch, ss in first ch to join.

Round 1: *5ch, ss in ring; rep from * a further three times, 3ch, 1trtr in ring.

Round 2: *3ch, ss in 5ch-sp; rep from * a further four times.

Round 3: *3ch, 2tr in same ch-sp, 2ch, *3tr in ch-sp, 2ch; rep from * around, ss in third ch of t-ch to join.

Round 5: *1ch, work 1dc in each st and 2dc in each ch-sp around, ss to first dc to join.

Round 7: *5ch, miss 1 st, ss in next stitch; rep from * around.

Fasten off.

Motif 4

Make 5ch, ss in first ch to join.

Round 1: *5ch, ss in ring; rep from * a further three times, 2ch, 1trtr in ring.

Round 2: *7ch, ss in third ch of 5ch-sp; rep from * a further three times,

3ch, 1trtr in third ch of 5ch-sp (at the base of 7ch).

Round 3: *5ch, ss in 4th ch of 7ch-sp; rep from * a further three times, 2ch, 1trtr in fourth ch of 5ch-sp (at the base of 7ch).

Rep Rounds 2 and 3 to make the motif as large as desired.

Finishing

I made three motifs per wing, but you can do as many or as few as you like. For one wing lay motifs 1, 2, and 3 inside your wing frame – the largest in the centre and the smaller two at either end.

Using the tapestry needle and a length of yarn, stitch the edges touching the frame in place to the frame covering. Repeat for the other wing using motifs 1, 2 and 4.

Using scraps of yarn, start at the frame edge, stitch in the gaps between the circles.

Straps

To make loops for the ribbon straps, work as follows:

For the right-hand wing only, join yarn at the top of the outside edge of the frame, *3ch, ss in next st; rep from * a further nine times. (10 loops made)

Rep for left-hand wing, lining the loops up to match the right-hand wing.

Take two lengths of ribbon and lace them between the wings into the loops as though you are lacing up shoes.

Cowboy Carl
(or Carla)

This is another one of those patterns that was in my head for ages and I was nervous about starting it, as I thought it might be really complicated. As it turned out, this was in fact all finished and done within a couple of hours and is one of the single most pleasing makes ever! The big beast loves wearing it, and the gun holster and badge were requests to make up a complete costume to play in. I'm extremely tempted to make a larger version of this hat for me to wear in the winter, and have already been asked by my sister if I can make one for her…and she is 34!

Complete the Look

A checked shirt, pair of jeans, and a belt are all you need to finish off this costume. If you happen to have a scrap of fabric lying around that would make a good neckerchief, then all the better.

Hat

SKILL LEVEL ★★

Yeehaw! I'm not quite sure if this is a Stetson or a Ten-Gallon, but every cowboy needs a hat.

Pattern Notes

The centre of the hat is made in double crochet stitches to give a sturdy shape to the middle of the hat. The remainder is worked in treble crochet stitches to keep the brim more flexible and easier to shape.

You will need

Yarn
Chunky weight:
100g (3½oz) of Tan

Hooks & Notions
5.5mm (US I/9) crochet hook
Tapestry needle

Tension
Tension is not critical but adjust the hook size to produce a firm fabric.

Size
One size: To fit 4-7years
53cm (21in) circumference

Abbreviations
See page 8.

For the Hat

Make 13ch.

Set-up: Work 2tr in fourth ch from hook, 1tr in next 8 sts, 5tr in end ch. Working up the other side of the foundation chain, 1tr in next 8 sts, 2tr in last st, ss in third ch of t-ch to join. (26 sts)

Working in the round, continue as follows:

Round 1: 3ch (counts as 1tr now and throughout), 2tr in next 2 sts, 1tr in next 8 sts, 2tr in next 2 sts, 1tr, 2tr in next 2 sts, 1tr in next 9 sts, 2tr in next 2 sts, ss in third ch of t-ch to join. (34 sts)

Round 2: 1ch, 1dc in each st around, ss in first dc to join. (34 sts)

Round 3: 1ch, 1dc, 2dc in next st, 1dc in next 14 sts, 2dc in next st, 1dc in next st, 2dc in next st, 1dc in next 14 sts, 2dc in next st, ss in first dc to join. (38 sts)

Round 4: 1ch, 1dc, 2dc in next st, 1dc in next 16 sts, 2dc in next st, 1dc in next st, 2dc in next st, 1dc in next 16 sts, 2dc in next st, ss in first dc to join. (42 sts)

Round 5: 1ch, 1dc, 2dc in next st, 1dc in next 18 sts, 2dc in next st, 1dc in next st, 2dc in next st, 1dc in next 18 sts, 2dc in next st, ss in first dc to join. (46 sts)

Round 6: 3ch, 1tr in each st around, ss in third ch of t-ch to join.

Round 7: 3ch, 1tr in next 18 sts, 2tr in next st, 1tr in next 6 sts, 2tr in next st, 1tr in next 19 sts, ss in third ch of t-ch to join. (48 sts)

Round 8: 3ch, 1tr in next 18 sts, 2tr in next st, 1tr in next 8 sts, 2tr in next st, 1tr in last 19 sts, ss in third ch of t-ch to join. (50 sts)

Round 9: 3ch, 1tr in next 2 sts, 2tr in next st, 1tr in next 42 sts, 2tr in next st, 1tr in last 3 sts, ss in third ch of t-ch to join. (52 sts)

Round 10: 3ch, 2tr in next st, 1tr in next 23 sts, 2tr in next st, 1tr in next st, 2tr in next st, 1tr in next 24 sts, ss in third ch of t-ch to join. (55 sts)

Rounds 11-14: 3ch, 1tr in each st around.

Round 15: 3ch, *1tr in next 5 sts, 2tr in next st; rep from * to end, ss in third ch of t-ch to join. (64 sts)

Round 16: 3ch, *1tr in next 6 sts, 2tr in next st; rep from * to end, ss in third ch of t-ch to join. (73 sts)

Round 17: 3ch, *1tr in next 7 sts, 2tr in next st; rep from * to end, ss in third ch of t-ch to join. (82 sts)

Round 18: 3ch, *1tr in next 8 sts, 2tr in next st; rep from * to end, ss in third ch of t-ch to join. (91 sts)

Round 19: 3ch, *1tr in next 9 sts, 2tr in next st; rep from * to end, ss in third ch of t-ch to join. (100 sts)
Fasten off.

Finishing

Weave in all loose ends. Using A, secure the sides of the brim to the hat at either side.

Shape the top of the hat by tucking the central double crochet area down into the middle a little bit and secure with a few stitches if required.

Holster

SKILL LEVEL ✷   This holster also makes a handy extra pocket.

You will need

Yarn

Chunky weight:
35g (1¼oz) of Tan

Hooks & Notions

5.5mm (US I/9) crochet hook

Tapestry needle

Belt to wear your holster on

Tension

Tension is not critical but
adjust the hook size to
produce a firm fabric.

Size

One size: 11.5cm (4½in) wide x
21.5cm (8½in) tall

Abbreviations

See page 8.

For the Holster

Make 19ch.

Row 1: 1dc in second ch from hook, 1dc in each ch to end, turn.
(18 sts)

Rows 2-3: 1ch, 1dc in each st to end, turn.

Row 4: 1ch, 2dc in next st, 1dc in next 16 sts, 2dc in last st, turn.
(20 sts)

Row 5: 1ch, 2dc in next st, 1dc in next 18 sts, 2dc in last st, turn.
(22 sts)

Rows 6-11: 1ch, 1dc in each st to end, turn.

Row 12: 1ch, dc2tog, 1dc in next 18 sts, dc2tog, turn. (20 sts)

Row 13: 1ch, 1dc in each st to end, turn.

Row 14: 1ch, 2dc in the next st, 1dc in next 18
sts, 2dc in last st, turn. (22 sts)

Row 15: 1ch, 1dc in each st to
end, turn.

Row 16: 1ch, 2dc in next
st, 1dc in next 20 sts,
2dc in last st, turn.
(24 sts)

Row 17: 1ch, 1dc in
each st to end, turn.

Row 18: 1ch, 2dc
in next st, 1dc in
next 22 sts, 2dc in
last st, turn. (26 sts)

Rows 19-22: 1ch, 1dc in each st to end, turn.

Row 23: 1ch, 2dc in next st, 1dc in next 24 sts, 2dc in last st, turn. (28 sts)

Row 24: 1ch, 2dc in next st, 1dc in next 26 sts, 2dc in the last st, turn. (30 sts)

Rows 25-26: 1ch, 1dc in each st to end, turn.

Row 27: 1ch, dc2tog, 1dc in next 18 sts, turn. Do not fasten off!

Work the belt loops as follows:

Rows 28-32: 1ch, 1dc in next 4 sts, turn.

Row 33: 1ch, 1dc in next 4 sts. Fasten off. One belt loop created.

Rows 34-39: Rejoin yarn to Row 27, one st along from the previous loop, and repeat Rows 28-33.

Rows 40-45: Repeat Rows 34-39. Fasten off.

Finishing

Weave in all loose ends. Fold fabric in half lengthwise and seam, creating a pocket for the Sheriff's gun.

Sheriff's Badge

SKILL LEVEL ✶✶　　If you want to keep the baddies out of Dodge, then you'll need a badge so everyone knows you're the sheriff.

You will need

Yarn
Chunky weight:
Small quantity of Light Grey

Hooks & Notions
5.5mm (US I/9) crochet hook
Tapestry needle
Safety pin

Tension
Tension is not critical but adjust the hook size to produce a firm fabric.

Size
One size: 6.5cm (2½in) wide from point to point

Abbreviations
See page 8.

For the Badge

Round 1: Leaving a long tail, make a magic ring and ss to secure. Work 6dc into ring, ss in first dc to join. (6 sts)

Round 2: 2dc in each st around. (12 sts)

Round 3: *4ch, ss in second ch from hook, 1dc in next st, 1htr in next st, miss 1 st, ss in next st; rep from * a further five times. Fasten off.

Finishing
Use the long tail from the magic ring to stitch the safety pin to the back of the badge. Weave in all loose ends.

Pattern Notes
To give the badge a metallic look, hold a strand of sparkly thread with the yarn as you work.

Red Riding Hood

Oddly, although a really simple and quick pattern, this is one of "those ones" that took ages to work out the best way to make it. I'd been asked by a friend if I could make a cape and this is the first thing that came to mind, but I spent months making and ripping back subtly different versions. I'd take it on the train, to the park, in the office on my lunch breaks, until finally I got it right. I think it's exceptionally cute and was well worth the work. The apple is one of the first amigurumi that I ever made and was a gift for a friend who had never seen woollen fruit before – she was extremely tickled to have it!

Complete the Look

Any pretty dress would look super cute with this little hood, whether in winter or summer.

Hooded Cape

SKILL LEVEL ✶ ✶ Super sweet and equally cosy, this can double up as a winter warmer, as well as a costume.

You will need

Yarn
Chunky weight:
150g (5¼oz) of Red

Hooks & Notions
7mm (US K/10½) crochet hook
Tapestry needle

Tension
Tension is not critical but adjust your hook to produce a flexible fabric.

Size
One size: To fit 4-7 years
Neck: 35cm (14in) circumference worn with 7.5cm (3in) positive ease
Length: 45cm (17¾in) from top of head to base of cape

Abbreviations
See page 8.

For the Cape

Row 1 (RS): Make 42ch, 1tr in fourth ch from hook, *1tr in next 5 ch, 2tr in next ch, miss next ch; rep from * a further four times, 1tr in last 3 ch, turn. (40 sts)

Row 2: 3ch (counts as 1tr now and throughout), *1tr in next 5 sts, 2tr in next st; rep from * a further five times, 1tr in last 3 sts, turn. (46 sts)

Row 3: 3ch, *1tr in next 6 sts, 2tr in next st; rep from * a further five times, 1tr in last 3 sts, turn. (52 sts)

Row 4: 3ch, *1tr in next 7 sts, 2tr in next st; rep from * a further five times, 1tr in last 3 sts, turn. (58 sts)

Row 5: 3ch, *1tr in next 8 sts, 2tr in next st; rep from * a further five times, 1tr in last 3 sts, turn. (64 sts)

Row 6: 3ch, *1tr in next 9 sts, 2tr in next st; rep from * a further five times, 1tr in last 3 sts, turn. (70 sts)

Row 7: 3ch, *1tr in next 10 sts, 2tr in next st; rep from * a further five times, 1tr in last 3 sts, 2ch, turn. (76 sts)

Row 8: 3ch, *1tr in next 11 sts, 2tr in next st; rep from * a further five times, 1tr in last 3 sts, turn. (82 sts)

Row 9: 3ch, *1tr in next 12 sts, 2tr in next st; rep from * a further five times, 1tr in last 3 sts, 2ch, turn. (88 sts)

Row 10: 3ch, *1tr in next 13 sts, 2tr in next st; rep from * a further five times, 1tr in last 3 sts, 2ch, ss in third ch of t-ch to finish. (94 sts)
Fasten off.

Pattern Notes

The main cape section is made first and the hood worked afterwards. If you prefer, the hood can be made separately and sewn on.

To fasten the cape you can leave long tails when starting, or alternatively thread a ribbon through the stitches for a fancier fastening.

For the Hood

With RS facing, rejoin yarn at the right-hand edge. Work into the starting chain of cape as follows:

Row 1 (RS): 3ch, 1tr in each st across, turn. (40 sts)

Row 2: 3ch, *1tr in next 5 sts, 2tr in next st; rep from * a further five times, 1tr in last 3 sts, turn. (46 sts)

Rows 3–17: 3ch, 1tr in each st to end, turn.

Row 18: 3ch, 1tr in each st across. Fasten off.

Finishing

Seam the top edges of the hood together.

Weave in all loose ends and block gently according to the ball band.

Use the remaining long tails to fasten around the neck. Alternatively, make chain lengths and attach to the cape or thread a ribbon through for a pretty finish.

Basket

SKILL LEVEL ★ ★

You will need

Yarn
Chunky weight:
25g (1oz) of Dark Brown

Hooks & Notions
5.5mm (US I/9) crochet hook
Removable stitch marker
Tapestry needle

Tension
Tension is not critical but
adjust your hook to produce
a firm fabric.

Size
One size:
30.5cm (12in) circumference
(at widest part);
23cm (9in) tall (including handle)

Abbreviations
See page 8.

This rustic-looking basket could be used by all sorts of fairytale characters, as well as Red Riding Hood.

Pattern Notes

The basket is worked on a small hook to give it strength and to hold the shape.

Use the stitch marker to indicate start of rounds when working in spirals, moving the stitch marker up as you progress.

For the Basket

Round 1: Make a magic ring and secure with ss. Work 6dc into ring, ss in first dc to join, pm. (6 sts)
Working in spirals, moving the marker up as you work, continue as follows:
Round 2: 2dc in each st to end. (12 sts)
Round 3: *2dc in next st, 1dc in next st; rep from * around. (18 sts)
Round 4: *2dc in next st, 1dc in next 2 sts; rep from * around. (24 sts)
Round 5: *2dc in next st, 1dc in next 3 sts; rep from * around. (30 sts)
Round 6: *2dc in next st, 1dc in next 4 sts; rep from * around. (36 sts)
Work in rounds as follows:
Round 7: 3ch, working in the back loop only 1tr in each st around, ss in third ch of t-ch to join. (36 sts)
Rounds 8-11: 3ch, 1tr in each st around, ss in third ch of t-ch to join. (36 sts)
Round 12: 1ch, 1dc in each st around.
Round 13: 1ch, working in the front loop only 1dc in each st around.
Do not fasten off and continue as follows to create the handle:
With hook still in ch from last round, make 31ch.
Miss 18 sts, ss into edge of basket to join handle to body of basket. 1ch, work dc back along the chain handle, ss back into body of the basket to finish.
Fasten off.

Finishing

Weave in all loose ends.

Apple

SKILL LEVEL ★★   A rosy red apple should make Grandma feel better – as long as the wolf doesn't eat it first.

You will need

Yarn
Chunky weight:
Small quantities of (**A**) Red, (**B**) Brown, and (**C**) Green

Hooks & Notions
5mm (US 8/H) crochet hook
Removable stitch marker
Small amount of toy stuffing
Tapestry needle

Tension
Tension is not critical but adjust your hook to produce a firm fabric.

Size
One size:
7cm (2¾in) high x 19.5cm (7¾in) circumference

Abbreviations
See page 8.

Pattern Notes
Use the stitch marker to indicate start of rounds when working in spirals, moving the stitch marker up as you progress.

For the Apple

Round 1: Using A, leaving a long tail, make a magic ring and ss to secure. Work 6dc into ring, pm. (6 sts)
Working in spirals, moving the marker up as you work, continue as follows:

Round 2: 2dc in each st around. (12 sts)

Round 3: *2dc in next st, 1dc in next st; rep from * around. (18 sts)

Round 4: *2dc in next st, 1dc in next 2 sts; rep from * around. (24 sts)

Round 5: *2dc in next st, 1dc in next 3 sts; rep from * around. (30 sts)

Rounds 6-11: 1dc in each st around.

Round 12: Dc2tog, 1dc in next 28 sts. (29 sts)

Round 13: 1dc in next 14 sts, dc2tog, 1dc in next 13 sts. (28 sts)

Round 14: 1dc in next 6 sts, dc2tog, 1dc in next 20 sts. (27 sts)

Round 15: 1dc in next 18 sts, dc2tog, 1dc in next 7 sts. (26 sts)

Round 16: Dc2tog, 1dc in next 24 sts. (25 sts)
Do not fasten off.
Pull tail from magic ring through and out of the bottom, gently stuff the apple taking care not to overfill it. Ensure the tail is still poking out of the bottom and continue as follows:

Round 17: *Dc2tog, 1dc in next 2 sts; rep from * to last st, 1dc. (19 sts)

Round 18: *Dc2tog, 1dc in next st; rep from * to last 4 sts, [dc2tog] twice. (12 sts)

Round 19: [Dc2tog] six times, ss in first dc to join.
Fasten off, leaving a long tail.
Make sure the magic ring tail is still poking through the bottom centre, then pull and tightly tie it together with the slip stitch tail to give the apple a lovely appley shape.
Weave in all loose ends.

For the Stalk

Using B and leaving a long tail, make 6ch, ss in second ch from hook, ss in next 4 sts.
Fasten off, leaving a long tail.

For the Leaf

Using C and leaving a long tail, make 7ch, 1dc in second ch from hook, 1htr in next ch, 1tr in next ch, 1htr in next ch, 1dc in next ch, ss in next ch. Rotate fabric, and work down the other side of the chain as follows: ss in first ch, 1dc in next ch, 1htr in next ch, 1tr in next ch, 1htr in next ch, 1dc in next ch, ss in last ch.
Fasten off, leaving a long tail.

Finishing

Using the tapestry needle, thread the long tails of the stalk and the leaf down from the top of the apple, through the centre, and out of the bottom. Tie together in a knot and then pull the threads back in and out of the apple at the side to weave in and trim.

Pussy Cat

This may sound a little macabre, but our cat is a little black and white sweetie called Treacle. A while ago she vanished for a few days, and while she turned up safely, her tail had gone missing. The big beast was a little upset by this and asked if we could get her a new one, so to placate him, I made one and told him that if Treacle wanted to, she could wear this one. Big beast was happy (and don't worry, Treacle is perfectly alright) and then small beast, who is very attached to the cat, asked if he could wear it. The mask then seemed the natural accompaniment.

Complete the Look

A simple black top with either leggings or tights is all you need to go with this. A really cute finishing touch would be to wear one white sock and one black sock to have little mismatched paws.

Hat

SKILL LEVEL ✶✶

This is such an easy costume to put on and purr about, it gets played with a lot by my boys and the neighbours' girls.

You will need

Yarn
Chunky weight:
50g (1¾oz) of Black

Hooks & Notions
5.5mm (US I/9) crochet hook
Tapestry needle

Tension
Tension is not critical but adjust the hook size to produce a firm fabric.

Size
One size: To fit 4-7 years
47cm (18½in) circumference

Abbreviations
See page 8.

Pattern Notes
Adjust the size to fit 2-3 years by omitting Round 4.

To make the hat in a larger size, use a US K/10½ (7mm) crochet hook, and omit Round 4.

For the Hat

Round 1: Using A, make a magic ring, secure with ss. 3ch (counts as 1tr now and throughout), work 11tr into ring, ss in third ch of t-ch to join. (12 sts)

Round 2: 3ch, 1tr in base of ch, 2tr in each st around, ss in third ch of t-ch to join. (24 sts)

Round 3: 3ch, 1tr in base of ch, 1tr in next st, *2tr in next st, 1tr in next st; rep from * around, ss in third ch of t-ch to join. (36 sts)

Round 4: 1ch, 1tr in base of ch, 1tr in next 2 sts, *2tr in next st, 1tr in next 2 sts; rep from * around, ss in third ch of t-ch to join. (48 sts)

Rounds 5-12: 3ch, 1tr in each st around, ss in third ch of t-ch to join.

Round 13 (eyehole round): 3ch, 1tr in next 10 sts, 1dtr in next st, 1trtr in next st, 10ch, miss 6 sts, 1trtr in next 3 sts, 10ch, miss 6 sts, 1trtr in next st, 1dtr in next st, 1tr in each st to end, ss in third ch of t-ch to join. (36 sts and two sets of 10ch-sp)

Round 14: 3ch, 1tr in each st to eyeholes, 8tr around the whole chain (rather than through the sts), 1tr in each st between the eyes, 8tr around second eyehole chain, 1tr in each of next 5 sts, tr2tog, 1tr in next 5 sts, tr2tog, 1tr in next 5 sts,

tr2tog, ss in third ch of t-ch to join. Fasten off.

For the Ears (make 2)

Make 8ch, ss in second ch from hook, 1dc in next ch, 1htr in next ch, 1dtr in next ch, 1trtr in next ch, 3ch, ss in end of ch. Working along the other side of the foundation chain, 3ch, 1trtr in next ch, 1dtr in next ch, 1tr in next ch, 1htr in next ch, 1dc in next ch, ss in last ch. Fasten off leaving a long tail.

Finishing

Attach ears in desired position. Weave in all loose ends.

Tail

SKILL LEVEL ✷✷   This white-tipped tail can be swished about in all sorts of ways.

You will need

Yarn
Chunky weight yarn:
25g (1oz) of (**A**) Black
Small quantity of (**B**) White

Hooks & Notions
5.5mm (US I/9) crochet hook
Removable stitch marker
Toy stuffing
Length of black ribbon
Matching sewing needle and thread
Tapestry needle

Tension
Tension is not critical but adjust the hook size to produce a firm fabric.

Size
One size: 33cm (13in) long

Abbreviations
See page 8.

For the Tail

Note: You will find it easiest to stuff the tail as you go by adding the stuffing every ten rounds.

Round 1: Using A, make a magic ring and secure with ss. Work 8dc into ring, ss in first dc to join, 1ch, pm. (8 sts)
Work in spirals as follows, moving the stitch marker up each round:

Rounds 2–42: 1dc in each st around. (8 sts)
Fasten off A, join B, and continue in spirals as follows:

Rounds 43–47: 1dc in each st around.

Round 48: [Dc2tog] four times, ensuring the stuffing is right to the end of the tail.
Fasten off and close the opening.
Weave in all loose ends.

Finishing

Stitch the black end of the tail securely to the mid-point of the ribbon and use for tying around the waist of your little kitten.

Magic Unicorn

I have an identical twin – yep, a proper one, and we have a lot of fun confusing the neighbours and children! This pattern is one that she begged me to make for her. I was reticent because let's face it, it's never going to be the easiest thing to make, but actually it came together really quickly, and there is something extremely pleasing about seeing a grown woman clapping her hands like a five-year-old when presented with something you've made.

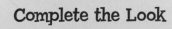

Complete the Look

I thought white leggings and a t-shirt would be good, but this is my sister's vision and she suggested a white leotard, white tights, and pink legwarmers – can you tell we grew up in the 1980s?!

Horn Headdress

SKILL LEVEL ✶✶ You can use any colour you like to make the mane and tail for this. I used two shades of pink, but you could do them all in grey for a boy.

Pattern Notes

Adjust the size to fit age 2–3 years by omitting Round 4.

You will need

Yarn

Chunky weight:
50g (1¾oz) of (**A**) White

DK (Light Worsted) weight:
25g (1oz) each of (**B**) White,
(**C**) Pale Pink, and (**D**) Neon Pink

Metallic 4ply (Fingering) weight:
Small quantity of (**E**) White or Silver

Note: If you can't find a metallic yarn, substitute it with an alternative 4ply (Fingering) weight yarn in a suitable colour.

Hooks & Notions

4mm (US G/6) crochet hook
5.5mm (US I/9) crochet hook
Removable stitch marker
Small amount of toy stuffing
Tapestry needle

Tension

Tension is not critical but adjust the hook size to produce a firm fabric.

Size

One size: To fit 4-7 years
47cm (18½in) circumference

Abbreviations

See page 8.

For the Hat

Round 1: Using A and 5.5mm (US I/9) hook, make a magic ring and secure with ss. 3ch (counts as 1tr now and throughout), work 11tr into ring, ss in third ch of t-ch to join. (12 sts)

Round 2: 3ch, 1tr in base of ch, 2tr in each st around, ss in third ch of t-ch to join. (24 sts)

Round 3: 3ch, 1tr at base of ch, 1tr in next st, *2tr in next st, 1tr in next st; rep from * to end, ss in third ch of t-ch to join. (36 sts)

Round 4: 3ch, 1tr at base of ch, 1tr in next 2 sts, *2tr in next st, 1tr in next 2 sts; rep from * to end, ss in third ch of t-ch to join. (48 sts)

Rounds 5–12: 3ch, 1tr in each st around, ss in third ch of t-ch to join. Continue as follows to make the chin-strap: *Make 62ch, 1tr in fourth ch from hook, 1tr in each ch back to the hat, ss in next 2 sts. Fasten off. Count 22 sts along, rejoin yarn, and rep from * once more.

For the Horn

Using B and E held together and 4mm (US G/6) hook, 3ch, ss in first ch to make a ring.
Working in spirals and using a stitch marker to indicate beginning of the round, continue as follows:

Round 1:
4dc into the ring. (4 sts)

Round 2: 2dc in first st, 1dc in next 3 sts. (5 sts)

Round 3: 1dc in next 2 sts, 2dc in next st, 1dc in next 2 sts. (6 sts)

Round 4: 2dc in first st, 1dc in next 5 sts. (7 sts)

Round 5: 1dc in next 3 sts, 2dc in next st, 1dc in next 3 sts. (8 sts)

Round 6: 2dc in first st, 1dc in next 7 sts. (9 sts)

Round 7: 1dc in next 4 sts, 2dc in next st, 1dc in next 4 sts. (10 sts)

Round 8: 2dc in first st, 1dc in next 9 sts. (11 sts)

Round 9: 1dc in next 5 sts, 2dc in next st, 1dc in next 5 sts. (12 sts)

Round 10: 2dc in first st, 1dc in next 11 sts. (13 sts)

Round 11: 1dc in next 6 sts, 2dc in next st, 1dc in next 6 sts. (14 sts)

Round 12: 2dc in first st, 1dc in next 13 sts. (15 sts)

Round 13: 1dc in next 7 sts, 2dc in next st, 1dc in next 7 sts. (16 sts)

Round 14: 2dc in first st, 1dc in next 15 sts, ss in first dc to join. (17 sts)
Fasten off.

For the Mane

Using C and D held together and 5.5mm (US I/9) hook, join yarn at middle point of the back of the hat edge. **Make 60ch, 1dc in second ch from hook, 1dc in each ch back to the hat, ss into hat one row above where you started**.
Following a line up the centre of the hat, 1dc in next row up and rep from ** to ** a further 8 times.
Work a further six lengths of mane repeating from ** to ** but reducing the number of starting chains by 5 each time. So for the next length make 55ch, the following make 50ch, and so on, finishing with a 35ch length.
Fasten off.

Finishing

Stuff the horn and sew to the centre front of the hat.
Weave in all ends.

Tail

SKILL LEVEL ✶ ✶

For a thicker tail, just crochet more strands until you run out of yarn.

You will need

Yarn

DK (Light Worsted) weight: Small quantity of (**A**) Pale Pink and (**B**) Neon Pink

Hooks & Notions

5.5mm (US I/9) crochet hook
Length of ribbon
Matching sewing needle and thread
Tapestry needle

Tension

Tension is not critical but adjust your hook to produce a flexible fabric.

Size

One size: 30.5cm (12in) long

Abbreviations

See page 8.

For the Tail

Using A and B held together, *make 60ch, 1dc in second ch from hook, 1dc in each ch to end; rep from * twice more.
Fasten off.

Finishing

Stitch the tail securely to the mid-point of the ribbon and use for tying around the waist of your little unicorn.

Vigo the Viking

One of my (many!) nephews is an utter sweetheart whose middle name is Thor. This costume collection was made purely for him, although the hammer has been pinched and used by all the family for general Thor-like purposes. The helmet sits up nice and high off the head, just to give it that extra Viking look.

Complete the Look

We made a really simple tabard to go with this outfit by cutting a hole for the head in the centre of a long rectangle of fabric. Pop a belt around it and ta-dah! You could just as easily use a big old t-shirt instead.

Helmet

SKILL LEVEL ★ ★

If you want to ward off blows from battle-axes and boulders, you need a stout Viking helmet to protect you.

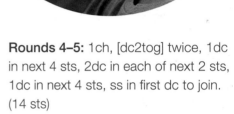

You will need

Yarn
Chunky weight:
100g (3½oz) of Grey (**A**)
Small quantity of White (**B**)

Hooks & Notions
7mm (US K/10½) crochet hook
Removable stitch marker
Small amount of toy stuffing
Tapestry needle

Tension
Tension is not critical but adjust the hook size to produce a firm fabric.

Size
One size: To fit 4-7 years
45.5cm (18in) circumference

Abbreviations
See page 8.

Pattern Notes
For a metallic effect, hold a strand of thin sparkly thread together with the grey as you work.

For the Helmet

Round 1: Using A, make a magic ring, secure with ss. Work 6dc into ring, ss in first dc to join, 1ch, pm. (6 sts)
Working in spirals, moving the marker up as you work, continue as follows:
Round 2: 2tr in each st around. (12 sts)
Round 3: *2tr in next st, 1tr in next st; rep from * a further five times. (18 sts)
Round 4: *2tr in next st, 1tr in next 2 sts; rep from * a further five times. (24 sts)
Round 5: *2tr in next st, 1tr in next 3 sts; rep from * a further five times. (30 sts)
Round 6: *2tr in next st, 1tr in next 4 sts; rep from * a further five times. (36 sts)
Rounds 7–16: 1tr in each st around.
Round 17: 1tr in each st around, ss in first tr to join.
Fasten off.

For the Horns (make 2)

Using B, make 14ch, ss in first ch to make a loop.
Rounds 1–3: 1ch, 1dc in each st around.

Rounds 4–5: 1ch, [dc2tog] twice, 1dc in next 4 sts, 2dc in each of next 2 sts, 1dc in next 4 sts, ss in first dc to join. (14 sts)
Round 6: 1ch, [dc2tog] three times, 1dc in next 2 sts st, [dc2tog] twice, 1dc in last 2 sts, ss in first dc to join. (9 sts)
Round 7: 1ch, [dc2tog] four times, 1dc in last st, ss in first dc to join. (5 sts)
Round 8: 1ch, [dc2tog] twice, 1dc in last st, ss in first dc to join. (2 sts)
Round 9: Dc2tog to close.
Fasten off, leaving a long tail that you can use to attach the horn to the hat. Fill with toy stuffing through the open end.

Finishing

Attach the horns to the helmet approximately 5cm (2in) from the bottom of the helmet on either side using the long tails.

Thor's Hammer

SKILL LEVEL ✱ ✱ This hammer is one of the most played with objects in our house, whether it's for being Thor, or just bashing each other!

You will need

Yarn
Chunky weight:
100g (3½oz) of (**A**) Grey
Small quantity of (**B**) Light Brown, and (**C**) Dark Brown

Hooks & Notions
5mm (US H/8) crochet hook
Small amount of toy stuffing
Removable stitch marker
Tapestry needle

Tension
Tension is not critical but adjust the hook size to produce a firm fabric.

Size
One size: 25cm (10in) from base of handle to top of hammer

Abbreviations
See page 8.

Pattern Notes
For a metallic effect, hold a strand of thin sparkly thread together with the grey as you work.

For the Hammer Head

Using A, make 22ch.
Rows 1-6: 1tr in third ch from hook, 1tr in each ch to end, turn. (20 sts)
Row 7: 3ch (counts as 1tr now and throughout), working in front loop only 1tr in each st to end, turn.
Rows 8-10: 3ch, 1tr in each st to end, turn.
Row 11: Repeat Row 7.
Rows 12-16: Repeat Row 8.
Rows 17-20: Repeat Rows 7-10.
Fasten off, leaving a long tail. Use the tail to sew the long edges together.

For the End Panels (make 2)

Using A, make 12ch.
Row 1: 1tr in third ch from hook and in each ch to end, turn. (10 sts)
Rows 2-6: 3ch (counts as a st now and throughout), 1tr in next 9 sts, turn. (10 sts)
Fasten off, leaving a long tail. Use the long tails to sew the end panels at either end and fill with toy stuffing before closing the second end panel.

For the Handle

Round 1: Using B and C held together, make a magic ring, secure with ss. Work 8dc into ring, ss in first dc to join, 1ch, pm. (8 sts)
Working in spirals, moving the marker up as you work, continue as follows:
Rounds 2-23: 1tr in each st around.
Ss in last tr to join and fasten off, leaving a long tail.

Finishing

Firmly stuff the handle and use the tail to attach the handle to the head. Weave in all loose ends.

Viking Cuffs

SKILL LEVEL ✱ These are made in brown yarn to look like the leather cuffs worn by real Viking warriors, to protect them in sword fights.

You will need

Yarn
DK (Light Worsted) weight:
50g (1¾oz) of (**A**) Brown
Small amount of (**B**) Grey

Hooks & Notions
5mm (US H/8) crochet hook
Tapestry needle

Tension
Tension is not critical
but the fabric should
be firm yet flexible.

Size
One size: To fit 4-7 years
16.5cm (6½in) circumference

Abbreviations
See page 8.

For the Cuffs (make 2)
Using A, make 26ch.
Row 1: 1dc in second ch from hook,
1dc in each ch to end, turn. (25 sts)
Rows 2–5: 1ch, 1dc in each st to
end, turn.
Fasten off, leaving a long tail.

Finishing
Using the long tails, sew the short
edges together. With B (and following
the photographs for guidance),
embroider three large crossed stitches
into the cuff.

Pattern Notes
You can easily make the cuffs
bigger or smaller by increasing
or reducing the number of
stitches in the beginning
chain, and adjusting the
number of rows you work.

Rapunzel

I have to confess that this was actually made just to please me, although it has proved extremely popular with all the little girls who come round to play! The chunky construction means it will stay looking lovely through many dress-up sessions. This really is one of those patterns that I wish I'd had when I was a little girl, because I honestly would have worn it until it fell apart! The shrug is one of the first things I learned to make and is so simple it's ridiculous! In fact, I have three of these that I wear on rotation all summer.

Complete the Look

A simple cotton summer dress is all you need for this, but if your Rapunzel happens to have a ball gown, then why not!

Hair

SKILL LEVEL ★ ★

The head part and the plaited hair of Rapunzel's wig are made in one continuous piece of crochet.

You will need

Yarn
Chunky weight :
50g (1¾oz) of (**A**) Bright Yellow, (**B**) Lemon Yellow, and (**C**) White

Hooks & Notions
8mm (US L/11) crochet hook
Tapestry needle

Tension
Tension is not critical but adjust the hook size to produce a firm fabric.

Size
One size: To fit 4-7 years
47cm (18½in) circumference

Abbreviations
See page 8.

Pattern Notes
Add flowers to Rapunzel's hair using elements from the Flower Garland Pattern on page 56 — make as many as you like and sew them on as desired.

For the Head

Round 1: Using A, B, and C held together, make a magic ring and secure with ss. 3ch (counts as 1tr now and throughout), 5tr into ring, ss in third ch of t-ch to join. (6 sts)

Round 2: 3ch, 1tr in base of ch, 2tr in each st to end, ss in third ch of t-ch to join. (12 sts)

Round 3: 3ch, 1tr in base of ch, 1tr in next st, *2tr in next st, 1tr in next st; rep from * a further four times, ss in third ch of t-ch to join. (18 sts)

Round 4: 3ch, 1tr in base of ch, 1tr in next 2 sts, *2tr in next st, 1tr in next 2 sts; rep from * a further four times, ss in third ch of t-ch to join. (24 sts)

Round 5: 3ch, 1tr in base of ch, 1tr in next 3 sts, *2tr in next st, 1tr in next 3 sts; rep from * a further four times, ss in third ch of t-ch to join. (30 sts)

Round 6: 3ch, 1tr in base of ch, 1tr in next 4 sts, *2tr in next st, 1tr in next 4 sts; rep from * a further four times, ss in third ch of t-ch to join. (36 sts)

Rounds 7-10: 3ch, 1tr in each st around, ss in third ch of t-ch to join.

For the Hair

**Using A, B, and C held together, make 92ch, 1tr in fourth ch from hook, 1tr in each ch, miss 2 sts on edge of hat, ss in next st to attach; rep from ** twice more.
Fasten off.
Working back and forth (without turning your work), create the hairline as follows:

Row 1: Rejoin yarn 10 sts from where the hair was fastened off. Make 16ch, miss 9 sts to the left, ss in next st of brim.

Row 2: 14ch, miss 8 sts to the right (next to where you started the fringe), ss in brim.

Row 3: 12ch, miss 7 sts to the right, ss in brim.

Row 4: 10ch, miss 6 sts to the left, ss in brim.

Row 5: 8ch, miss 5 sts to the right, ss in brim.

Row 6: 6ch, miss 4 sts to the left, ss in brim.
Fasten off.

Rejoin yarn where you originally started the hairline and work as follows:

Row 1: 8ch, miss 4 sts to the left, ss in brim.

Row 2: 6ch, miss 4 sts to the left, ss in brim.

Row 3: 5ch, miss 3 sts to the right, ss in brim.
Fasten off.

Finishing

Weave in all loose ends.
Plait the three hair strands and secure with a few stitches to keep them plaited together.
Add flowers as desired – see pattern notes for details.

Shrug

SKILL LEVEL ★★★ A pretty pink shrug completes Rapunzel's costume, but would work just as well with any princess outfit.

You will need

Yarn

DK (Light Worsted) weight:
50g (1¾oz) of Pink

Hooks & Notions

4mm (US G/6) crochet hook
Tapestry needle

Tension

Tension is not critical but the fabric should be flexible.

Size

One size: To fit 4-7 years
51 x 23cm (20 x 9in) before seaming

Abbreviations

See page 8.

For the Shrug

Row 1 (RS): Make 73ch, work 2tr in fifth ch from hook, 1ch, 2tr in next ch, *miss 3 ch, 2tr in next ch, 1ch, 2tr in next ch; rep from * to last 2 ch, miss 1 ch, 1tr in last ch, turn.

Row 2: 3ch, miss 2 sts, [2tr, 1ch, 2tr] in 1ch-sp from previous row, *miss 4 sts, [2tr, ch 1, 2tr] in 1ch-sp from previous row; rep from * to last 2 sts, miss 2 sts, 1tr in third ch of t-ch, turn.

Rows 3–19: Repeat Row 2. Fasten off.

Finishing

Weave in loose ends and gently block the rectangle according to the ball band instructions.

Lay the piece flat with right side of fabric facing. Fold in half, so the longer edges meet and the wrong side is now facing you.

Working from the outside in (along the long edge), seam approximately 2.5cm (1in) on the right-hand side to create an armhole.

Repeat for the other side.

Fasten off. Weave in all ends.

Wicked Witch

Having made the snowflake collar for the Snow Queen outfit on page 38, the next thing to pop into my head was a cobweb collar, so this costume actually started at the neck and worked its way up to the hat. The geek in me wanted a perfect cone for the hat, so while there are other more traditional ways to crochet a cone, this one takes a little more concentration but the outcome is really good and worth the extra effort.

Complete the Look

Well really you should have hobnail boots, a cape made of the night sky, and a dress woven from pure darkness, but if you don't have those around the house then some stripy tights and old black clothes will do nicely!

Hat

SKILL LEVEL ★★ Every witch needs a hat, under which she can hide frogs, newts, and anything else she needs to keep handy for her cauldron.

You will need

Yarn

Chunky weight:
100g (3½oz) of Black

Hooks & Notions

5.5mm (US I/9) crochet hook

Removable stitch marker

Tapestry needle

Tension

Tension is not critical but adjust the hook size to produce a firm fabric.

Size

One size: To fit 4-7 years
50cm (19½in) circumference (excluding brim);
29cm (11½in) tall

Abbreviations

See page 8.

Pattern Notes

The rounds of treble crochet toward the base of the hat provide a bit more stretch, making the hat comfier and more secure to wear.

For the Hat

Make 3ch, ss in first ch to make a ring.

Working in spirals, moving the marker up as you work, continue as follows:

Round 1: 4dc into the ring, pm. (4 sts)

Round 2: *2dc in next st, 1dc in next st; rep from * around. (6 sts)

Round 3: *2dc in next st, 1dc in next 2 sts; rep from * around. (8 sts)

Round 4: 1dc in next 2 sts, 2dc in next st, 1dc in next 3 sts, 2dc in next st, 1dc in next st. (10 sts)

Round 5: 1dc in next st, 2dc in next st, 1dc in next 4 sts, 2dc in next st, 1dc in next 3 sts. (12 sts)

Round 6: 1dc in next 4 sts, 2dc in next st, 1dc in next 5 sts, 2dc in next st, 1dc in next st. (14 sts)

Round 7: 2dc in next st, 1dc in next 6 sts, 2dc in next st, 1dc in next 6 sts. (16 sts)

Round 8: 1dc in next 4 sts, 2dc in next st, 1dc in next 7 sts, 2dc in next st, 1dc in next 3 sts. (18 sts)

Round 9: 1dc in next 8 sts, 2dc in next st, 1dc in next 8 sts, 2dc in next st. (20 sts)

Round 10: 1dc in next 2 sts, 2dc in next st, 1dc in next 9 sts, 2dc in next st, 1dc in next 7 sts. (22 sts)

Round 11: 1dc in next 6 sts, 2dc in next st, 1dc in next 10 sts, 2dc in next st, 1dc in next 4 sts. (24 sts)

Round 12: 2dc in next st, 1dc in next 11 sts, 2dc in next st, 1dc in next 11 sts. (26 sts)

Round 13: 1dc in next 5 sts, 2dc in next st, 1dc in next 12 sts, 2dc in next st, 1dc in next 7 sts. (28 sts)

Round 14: 1dc in next 11 sts, 2dc in next st, 1dc in next 13 sts, 2dc in next st, 1dc in next 2 sts. (30 sts)

Round 15: 1dc in next 4 sts, 2dc in next st, 1dc in next 14 sts, 2dc in next st, 1dc in next 10 sts. (32 sts)

Round 16: 2dc in next st, 1dc in next 15 sts, 2dc in next st,

1dc in next 15 sts. (34 sts)

Round 17: 1dc in next 10 sts, 2dc in next st, 1dc in next 16 sts, 2dc in next st, 1dc in next 6 sts. (36 sts)

Round 18: 1dc in next 3 sts, 2dc in next st, 1dc in next 17 sts, 2dc in next st, 1dc in next 14 sts. (38 sts)

Round 19: 1dc in next 15 sts, 2dc in next st, 1dc in next 18 sts, 2dc in next st, 1dc in next 14 sts. (40 sts)

Round 20: 1dc in next 9 sts, 2dc in next st, 1dc in next 19 sts, 2dc in next st, 1dc in next 10 sts. (42 sts)

Round 21: 1dc in next st, 2dc in next st, 1dc in next 20 sts, 2dc in next st, 1dc in next 19 sts. (44 sts)

Round 22: 1dc in next 16 sts, 2dc in next st, 1dc in next 21 sts, 2dc in next st, 1dc in next 5 sts. (46 sts)

Round 23: 1dc in next 8 sts, 2dc in next st, 1dc in next 22 sts, 2dc in next st, 1dc in next 14 sts. (48 sts)

Round 24: 1dc in next 23 sts, 2dc in next st, 1dc in next 23 sts, 2dc in next st. (50 sts)

Round 25: 1dc in next 16 sts, 2dc in next st, 1dc in next 24 sts, 2dc in next st, 1dc in next 8 sts. (52 sts)

Round 26: 1dc in next 8 sts, 2dc in next st, 1dc in next 25 sts, 2dc in next st, 1dc in next 17 sts. (54 sts)

Round 27: 2dc in next st, 1dc in next 26 sts, 2dc in next st, 1dc in next 26 sts. (56 sts)

Round 28: 1dc in next 17 sts, 2dc in next st, 1dc in next 27 sts, 2dc in next st, 1dc in next 10 sts. (58 sts)

Round 29: 1dc in next 7 sts, 2dc in next st, 1dc in next 28 sts, 2dc in next st, 1dc in next 21 sts. (60 sts)

Working in rounds, continue as follows:

Rounds 30-34: 3ch (counts as 1tr), 1tr in each st around.

Working in spirals again, continue as follows for the brim:

Round 35: For this round only, work into the front loop of each st as follows: *1dc in next 9 sts, 2dc in next st; rep from * a further five times. (66 sts)

Round 36: *1dc in next 10 sts, 2dc in next st; rep from * a further five times. (72 sts)

Round 37: *1dc in next 11 sts, 2dc in next st; rep from * a further five times. (78 sts)

Round 38: *1dc in next 12 sts, 2dc in next st; rep from * a further five times. (84 sts)

Round 39: *1dc in next 13 sts, 2dc in next st; rep from * a further five times. (90 sts)

Round 40: *1dc in next 14 sts, 2dc in next st; rep from * a further five times. (96 sts)

Fasten off.

Finishing

Weave in all loose ends and let the brim curl up slightly.

Stand back and admire the beautiful cone!

Cobweb Collar

SKILL LEVEL ✷✷ This cute little collar would look just as good on an adult, as part of a Halloween costume.

You will need

Yarn
DK (Light Worsted) weight: Small quantity of Black

Hooks & Notions
4mm (US G/6) crochet hook
75cm (30in) black ribbon
Tapestry needle

Tension
Tension is not critical but adjust your hook to produce a firm fabric.

Size
One size: 37.5cm (15in) wide (excluding ribbon)

Abbreviations
See page 8.

Pattern Notes
Adjust the size of the collar by adding more or fewer cobwebs and altering the length of the ribbon.

Hold a strand of silver metallic embroidery thread together with the yarn as you work to make sparkly cobwebs.

For the Cobweb Motif (make 5)

Round 1: Make a magic ring and secure with ss. Work 5dc into ring, ss in first dc to join, pm. (5 sts)

Round 2: *Make 11ch, ss in second ch from hook and each ch back to dc, ss in next st; rep from * a further four times. Five "spokes" created. Fasten off.

Round 3: Starting from the centre circle, count up 2 sts on one of your previous 11ch spokes, rejoin yarn, *3ch, and then ss into second stitch up of the next 11ch spoke; rep from * a further four times.

Round 4: Starting from the centre circle, count up 6 sts on one of your previous 11ch spokes, rejoin yarn, *6ch, and then ss into sixth st up of your next 11ch spoke; rep from * a further four times. Fasten off.

Round 5: Starting from the centre circle, count up 8 sts on one of your previous 11ch spokes, rejoin yarn, *11ch, and then ss into eighth st up of your next 11ch spoke; rep from * a further four times. Fasten off leaving a long tail.

Finishing
Lay the five motifs out so one side from each is touching the next one and sew them together. Weave in all loose ends. Thread the ribbon through either side of the cobweb panel and tie in a bow around your witch's neck.

Spider

SKILL LEVEL ✷✷ An amigurumi spider completes the costume
– a vital ingredient for casting spells.

You will need

Yarn

DK (Light Worsted) weight:
Small quantity of Black

Hooks & Notions

4mm (US G/6) crochet hook
Removable stitch marker
Toy stuffing
Silver embroidery thread
Embroidery needle
Tapestry needle

Tension

Tension is not critical
but adjust the hook size
to produce a firm fabric.

Size

One size: 3cm (1¼in)
excluding legs

Abbreviations

See page 8.

For the Body

Round 1: Make a magic ring and secure with ss. Work 6dc into ring, ss in first dc to join, pm. (6 sts)
Working in spirals and using a stitch marker to indicate beginning of the round, continue as follows:
Round 2: 2dc in each st around. (12 sts)
Round 3: *2dc in next st, 1dc in next st; rep from * a further five times. (18 sts)
Round 4: 1dc in each st around.
Round 5: *Dc2tog, 1dc in next st; rep from * a further five times. (12 sts)
Stuff the spider and continue as follows:
Round 5: *Dc2tog; rep from * a further five times. (6 sts)
Fasten off and close the end.

For the Legs (make 8)

Make 8ch.
Fasten off, leaving a long tail.

Finishing

Sew the legs to the body. Weave in all loose ends.
Use the silver embroidery thread to stitch a little face on and pull the thread up through the top of his body to make a long thread to dangle it from. He can either be attached to the tip or brim of the hat, hung from the collar, or just be sat on a shoulder to give people a fright!

Wily Wizard

There's a funny old book from the 1970s called *Melric the Magician who Lost His Magic,* which my eldest son loves! Melric wears a red and yellow hat, in fact his whole outfit is red with yellow stars, and so a red and yellow wizard hat was requested for wearing to World Book Day at school. Abracadabra! My son came home with the "best costume" prize – I think I was probably more excited than he was!

Complete the Look

You could just wear an oversized t-shirt with a belt around the middle and jogging bottoms, or an old dressing gown, but if you want to go all out and create a real showstopper, embellish the clothing with printed stars. Cut a potato in half and carve a star shape into it. Using fabric paint, let the kids go wild stamping stars on to the t-shirt or dressing gown. Leave the garment to dry thoroughly and ta-dah!

Hat

SKILL LEVEL ✶✶   Abracadabra! You could make this hat up in any colour you like, but red is our favourite.

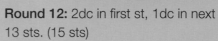

You will need

Yarn
Chunky weight:
75g (2¾oz) of (**A**) Red

DK (Light Worsted) weight:
Small quantity of (**B**) Yellow

Hooks & Notions
5.5mm (US I/9) crochet hook
4mm (US G/6) crochet hook
Removable stitch marker
Tapestry needle

Tension
Tension is not critical but adjust the hook size to produce a firm fabric.

Size
One Size: To fit 4-7 years, 48cm (19½in) circumference; 39.5cm(15½in) tall

Abbreviations
See page 8.

Pattern Notes
Make stars of different sizes by using a thicker or thinner yarn and adjusting your hook accordingly.

Hold a strand of metallic thread together with the yarn for a sparkly and magical finish.

For the Hat

Using A and 5.5mm (US I/9) hook, make 3ch, ss in first ch to make a ring. Working in spirals and, using a stitch marker to indicate beginning of the round, continue as follows:

Round 1: 4dc into the ring. (4 sts)

Round 2: 2dc in first st, 1dc in next 3 sts. (5 sts)

Round 3: 1dc in next 2 sts, 2dc in next st, 1dc in next 2 sts. (6 sts)

Round 4: 2dc in first st, 1dc in next 5 sts. (7 sts)

Round 5: 1dc in next 3 sts, 2dc in next st, 1dc in next 3 sts. (8 sts)

Round 6: 2dc in first st, 1dc in next 7 sts. (9 sts)

Round 7: 1dc in next 4 sts, 2dc in next st, 1dc in next 4 sts. (10 sts)

Round 8: 2dc in first st, 1dc in next 9 sts. (11 sts)

Round 9: 1dc in next 5 sts, 2dc in next st, 1dc in next 5 sts. (12 sts)

Round 10: 2dc in first st, 1dc in next 11 sts. (13 sts)

Round 11: 1dc in next 6 sts, 2dc in next st, 1dc in next 6 sts. (14 sts)

Round 12: 2dc in first st, 1dc in next 13 sts. (15 sts)

Round 13: 1dc in next 7 sts, 2dc in next st, 1dc in next 7 sts. (16 sts)

Round 14: 2dc in first st, 1dc in next 15 sts. (17 sts)

Round 15: 1dc in next 8 sts, 2dc in next st, 1dc in next 8 sts. (18 sts)

Round 16: 2dc in first st, 1dc in next 17 sts. (19 sts)

Round 17: 1dc in next 9 sts, 2dc in next st, 1dc in next 9 sts. (20 sts)

Round 18: 2dc in first st, 1dc in next 19 sts. (21 sts)

Round 19: 1dc in next 10 sts, 2dc in next st, 1dc in next 10 sts. (22 sts)

Round 20: 2dc in first st, 1dc in next 21 sts. (23 sts)

Round 21: 1dc in next 11 sts, 2dc in next st, 1dc in next 11 sts. (24 sts)

Round 22: 2dc in first st, 1dc in next 23 sts. (25 sts)

Round 23: 1dc in next 12 sts, 2dc in next st, 1dc in next 12 sts. (26 sts)

Round 24: 2dc in first st, 1dc in next 25 sts. (27 sts)

Round 25: 1dc in next 13 sts, 2dc in next st, 1dc in next 13 sts. (28 sts)

Round 26: 2dc in first st, 1dc in next 27 sts. (29 sts)

Round 27: 1dc in next 14 sts, 2dc in next st, 1dc in next 14 sts. (30 sts)

Round 28: 2dc in first st, 1dc in next 29 sts. (31 sts)

Round 29: 1dc in next 15 sts, 2dc in next st, 1dc in next 15 sts. (32 sts)

Round 30: 2dc in first st, 1dc in next 31 sts. (33 sts)

Round 31: 1dc in next 16 sts, 2dc in next st, 1dc in next 16 sts. (34 sts)

Round 32: 2dc in first st, 1dc in next 33 sts. (35 sts)

Round 33: 1dc in next 17 sts, 2dc in next st, 1dc in next 17 sts. (36 sts)

Round 34: 2dc in first st, 1dc in next 35 sts. (37 sts)

Round 35: 1dc in next 18 sts, 2dc in next st, 1dc in next 18 sts. (38 sts)

Round 36: 2dc in first st, 1dc in next 37 sts. (39 sts)

Round 37: 1dc in next 19 sts, 2dc in next st, 1dc in next 19 sts. (40 sts)

Round 38: 2dc in first st, 1dc in next 39 sts. (41 sts)

Round 39: 1dc in next 20 sts, 2dc in next st, 1dc in next 20 sts. (42 sts)

Round 40: 2dc in first st, 1dc in next 41 sts. (43 sts)

Round 41: 1dc in next 21 sts, 2dc in next st, 1dc in next 21 sts. (44 sts)

Round 42: 2dc in first st, 1dc in next 43 sts. (45 sts)

Round 43: 1dc in next 22 sts, 2dc in next st, 1dc in next 22 sts. (46 sts)

Round 44: 2dc in first st, 1dc in next 45 sts. (47 sts)

Round 45: 1dc in next 23 sts, 2dc in next st, 1dc in next 23 sts. (48 sts)

Round 46: 2dc in first st, 1dc in next 47 sts. (49 sts)

Round 47: 1dc in next 24 sts, 2dc in next st, 1dc in next 24 sts. (50 sts)

Round 48: 2dc in first st, 1dc in next 49 sts. (51 sts)

Round 49: 1dc in next 25 sts, 2dc in next st, 1dc in next 25 sts. (52 sts)

Round 50: 2dc in first st, 1dc in next 51 sts. (53 sts)

Round 51: 1dc in next 26 sts, 2dc in next st, 1dc in next 26 sts. (54 sts)

Round 52: 2dc in first st, 1dc in next 53 sts. (55 sts)

Round 53: 1dc in next 27 sts, 2dc in next st, 1dc in next 27 sts, ss in first dc to finish. (56 sts)
Fasten off.

For the Stars (make 7)

Using B and the 4mm (US G/6) hook, make 3ch, ss in first ch to join.

Round 1: 1ch, 10dc in ring, ss in first dc to join. (10 sts)

Round 2: *5ch, ss in second ch from hook, 1dc in next ch, 1hdc in next ch, 1tr in last ch, miss 1 st, ss in next st; rep from * a further four times.
Fasten off, leaving a long tail.

Finishing

Using the long tails, stitch the stars onto the hat.
Weave in all loose ends.

Beard

From Merlin to Melric, a beard is an essential part of the wizard's appearance.

You will need

Yarn
DK (Light Worsted) weight: Small quantity of White

Hooks & Notions
4mm (US G/6) crochet hook
Tapestry needle

Tension
Tension is not critical but adjust the hook size to produce a firm fabric.

Size
One size: To fit 4-7 years
19cm (7½in) wide, 16.5cm (6½in) tall (including moustache)

Abbreviations
See page 8.

For the Moustache

Leaving a long tail, make 30ch.
Row 1: Ss in second ch from hook, 1dc in next ch, 1hdc in next 2 ch, 1tr in next 2 ch, 1dtr in next 2 ch, 1trtr in next 2 ch, 1dtr in next ch, 1tr in next ch, 1hdc in next ch, 1dc in next ch, ss in next ch, 1dc in next ch, 1hdc in next ch, 1tr in next ch, 1dtr in next ch, 1trtr in next 2 ch, 1dtr in next 2 ch, 1tr in next 2 ch, 1hdc in next 2 ch, 1dc in next ch, ss in last ch to finish.
Fasten off, leaving a long tail.

For the Beard

Leaving a long tail, make 22ch.
Row 1: 1tr in fourth ch from hook, 1tr in next 8 ch, 3tr in next ch, 1tr in next 10 ch, turn. (20 sts)
Rows 2-4: 1ch, 1dc in each st to end, turn. (20 sts)
Row 5: 1ch, miss 1 st, 1dc in next 18 sts, miss 1 st, ss in last st, turn. (18 sts)
Row 6: 1ch, miss 1 st, 1dc in next 16 sts, miss 1 st, ss in last st, turn. (16 sts)
Row 7: 1ch, miss 1 st, 1dc in next 14 sts, miss 1 st, ss in last st, turn. (14 sts)
Row 8: 1ch, miss 1 st, 1dc in next 12 sts, miss 1 st, ss in last st, turn. (12 sts)
Rows 9-12: 1ch, 1dc in each st to end, turn. (12 sts)
Row 13: 1ch, miss 1 st, 1dc in next 10 sts, miss 1 st, ss in last st, turn. (10 sts)
Row 14: 1ch, miss 1 st, 1dc in next 8 sts, miss 1 st, ss in last st, turn. (8 sts)
Row 15: 1ch, miss 1 st, 1dc in next 6 sts, miss 1 st, ss in last st, turn. (6 sts)
Row 16: 1ch, miss 1 st, 1dc in next 4 sts, miss 1 st, ss in last st, turn. (4 sts)

Finishing

Using the long tails from the beard, sew the corners of the beard to the moustache and tie the long tails on the moustache to make loops to hook over the little wizard's ears.

Grey Rabbit

My smallest beast isn't a big hat wearer, even when there's snow up to your knees, so this was an attempt to get him into a hat he would be happy with! Any of you out there with stubborn, fashion-conscious creatures will know this was doomed to fail, but what it left us with was a costume to add to the dressing up box that is coveted by the little girl over the road, and worn on a weekly basis.

Complete the Look

We struggle to find plain tops, so invariably wear an inside-out grey top (usually with some sort of space ship on the outside!) and a pair of tracksuit bottoms. Anything pink or fluffy also works.

Hat

An excellent costume for Easter, this hat and the tail are brought out every March, and have even been taken to school.

You will need

Yarn
Chunky weight:
65g (2¼oz) of (**A**) Light Grey
Small quantities of (**B**) White, and (**C**) Pink

Hooks & Notions
5.5mm (US I/9) crochet hook
Tapestry needle

Tension
Tension is not critical but adjust the hook size to produce a firm fabric.

Size
One size: To fit 4-7 years, 47cm (18½in) circumference

Abbreviations
See page 8.

Pattern Notes
Adjust the size to fit 2-3 years by omitting Round 4.

To make the hat in a larger size, use a 7mm (US K/10½) crochet hook and omit Round 4.

For the Hat

Round 1: Using A, make a magic ring and secure with ss. 3ch (counts as 1tr now and throughout), work 11tr into ring, ss in third ch of t-ch to join. (12 sts)

Round 2: 3ch, 1tr in base of ch, 2tr in each st around, ss in third ch of t-ch to join. (24 sts)

Round 3: 3ch, 1tr at base of ch, 1tr in next st, *2tr in next st, 1tr in next st; rep from * to end, ss in third ch of t-ch to join. (36 sts)

Round 4: 3ch, 1tr at base of ch, 1tr in next 2 sts, *2tr in next st, 1tr in next 2 sts; rep from * to end, ss in third ch of t-ch to join. (48 sts)

Rounds 5-12: 3ch, 1tr in each st around, ss in third ch of t-ch to join.

Round 13 (eyehole round): 3ch, 1tr in next 13 sts, 1dtr in next st, 1trtr in next st, 10ch, miss 6 sts, 1trtr in next 2 sts, 10ch, miss 6 sts, 1trtr in next st, 1dtr in next st, 1tr in each st to end, ss in third ch of t-ch to join. (36 sts and two sets of 10ch-sp)

Round 14: 3ch, 1tr in next 13 sts, work 8tr around the chain (rather than through the sts), 1tr in each st between the eyes, 8tr around second chain, 1tr in each of next 10 sts, tr2tog, 2tr. Fasten off A.

Round 15: Join B at any st, ss around the edge, ss to join.
Fasten off. Weave in ends.

For the Nose

Using C, make 3ch.
Work 2tr in third ch from hook.
Fasten off. Sew to the middle stitches between the eyes as shown.

For the Ears (make 2)

Using A, make 16ch, ss in first ch from hook, 1dc in next ch, 1hdc in next ch, 1tr in next 10 ch, 3ch, ss in last ch.
Working along the opposite side of the foundation ch, continue as follows:
3ch, miss 1 ch, 1tr in next 10 ch, 1hdc in next ch, 1dc in next ch, ss in next ch to finish.
Fasten off, leaving a long tail.

Tail

SKILL LEVEL ✷ ✷   A little white tail puts the finishing touch to the rabbit outfit.

You will need

Yarn

Chunky weight:
25g (1oz) in White

Hooks & Notions

4mm (US G/6) crochet hook

Removable stitch marker

Small quantity of toy stuffing

Length of matching ribbon

Matching sewing needle and thread

Tapestry needle

Tension

Tension is not critical but adjust the hook size to produce a firm fabric.

Size

One size: 10cm (4in) diameter; 6cm (2½in) high

Abbreviations

See page 8.

For the Tail

Round 1: Using A, make a magic ring and secure with ss. Work 6dc into ring, ss in first dc to join, 1ch, pm. (6 sts) Work in spirals as follows, moving the stitch marker up each round:

Round 2: 2dc in each st around. (12 sts)

Round 3: *2dc in next st, 1dc in next st; rep from * a further five times. (18 sts)

Round 4: *2dc in next st, 1dc in next 2 sts; rep from * a further five times. (24 sts)

Rounds 5-10: 1dc in each st around.

Round 11: *Dc2tog, 1dc in next 2 sts; rep from * a further five times. (18 sts)

Round 12: *Dc2tog, 1dc in next st; rep from * a further five times. (12 sts)

Firmly stuff the tail and continue as follows:

Round 13: [Dc2tog] six times. (6 sts)

Round 14: [Dc2tog] three times, ss in first dc to join. Fasten off.

Finishing

Weave in all loose ends.

Stitch the tail securely at the mid-point of the ribbon and tie the tail in place on your little bunny and watch them hop away!

Techniques

In this section, we explain how to master the simple crochet and sewing techniques that you need to make the projects in this book.

BASIC CROCHET TECHNIQUES

Holding the hook

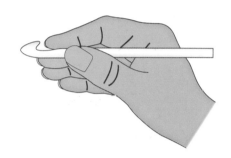

Holding the yarn

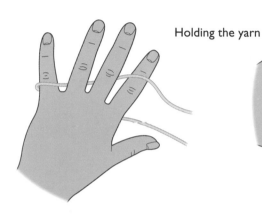

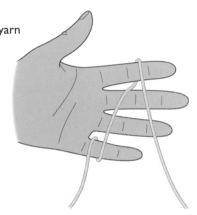

Pick up your hook as though you are picking up a pen or pencil. Keeping the hook held loosely between your fingers and thumb, turn your hand so that the palm is facing up and the hook is balanced in your hand and resting in the space between your index finger and your thumb.

1. Pick up the yarn with your little finger in the opposite hand to your hook, with your palm facing upward and with the short end in front. Turn your hand to face downward, with the yarn on top of your index finger and under the other two fingers and wrapped right around the little finger, as shown above.

2. Turn your hand to face you, ready to hold the work in your middle finger and thumb. Keeping your index finger only at a slight curve, hold the work or the slip knot using the same hand, between your middle finger and your thumb and just below the crochet hook and loop/s on the hook.

Making a slip knot
The simplest way is to make a circle with the yarn, so that the loop is facing downward.

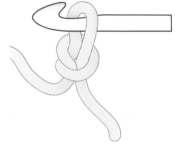

1. In one hand hold the circle at the top where the yarn crosses, and let the tail drop down at the back so that it falls across the centre of the loop. With your free hand or the tip of a crochet hook, pull a loop through the circle.

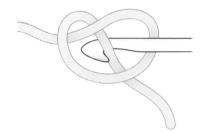

2. Put the hook into the loop and pull gently so that it forms a loose loop on the hook.

Yarn round hook (yrh)

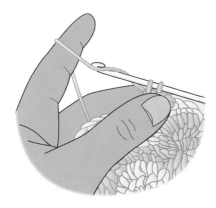

To create a stitch, catch the yarn from behind with the hook pointing upward. As you gently pull the yarn through the loop on the hook, turn the hook so it faces downward and slide the yarn through the loop. The loop on the hook should be kept loose enough for the hook to slide through easily.

Magic ring

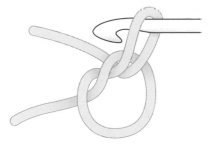

This is a useful starting technique if you do not want a visible hole in the centre of your round. Loop the yarn around your finger, insert the hook through the ring, yarn round hook, and pull through the ring to make the first chain. Work the number of stitches required into the ring and then pull the end to tighten the centre ring.

Chain (ch)

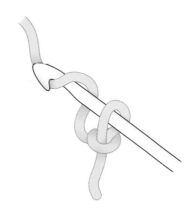

1. Using the hook, wrap the yarn over the hook ready to pull it through the loop on the hook.

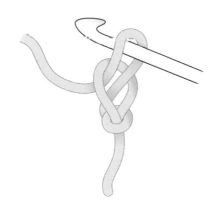

2. Pull through, creating a new loop on the hook. Continue in this way to create a chain of the required length.

Chain ring

If you are crocheting a round shape, one way of starting off is by crocheting a number of chains following the instructions in your pattern, and then joining them into a circle.

1. To join the chain into a circle, insert the crochet hook into the first chain that you made (not into the slip knot), yarn round hook.

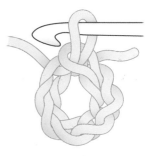

2. Pull the yarn through the chain and through the loop on your hook at the same time, thereby creating a slip stitch and forming a circle. You now have a chain ring ready to work stitches into as instructed in the pattern.

Chain space (ch-sp)

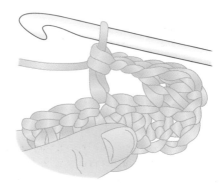

1. A chain space is the space that has been made under a chain in the previous round or row, and falls in between other stitches.

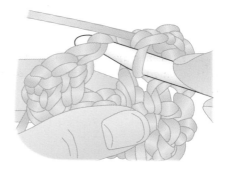

2. Stitches into a chain space are made directly into the hole created under the chain and not into the chain stitches themselves.

Making rounds

When working in rounds the work is not turned, so you are always working from one side. Depending on the pattern you are working, a "round" can be square. Start each round by making one or more chains to create the height you need for the stitch you are working:

Double crochet = 1 chain

Half treble crochet = 2 chains

Treble crochet = 3 chains

Work the required stitches to complete the round. At the end of the round, slip stitch into the top of the chain to close the round.

If you work in a spiral you do not need a turning chain. After completing your base ring, place a stitch marker in the first stitch and then continue to crochet around. When you have made a round and reached the point where the stitch marker is, work this stitch, take out the stitch marker from the previous round and put it back into the first stitch of the new round. A safety pin or piece of yarn in a contrasting colour is a good stitch marker.

Making rows

When making straight rows you turn the work at the end of each row and make a turning chain to create the height you need for the stitch you are working with, as for Making rounds.

Slip stitch (ss)

A slip stitch doesn't create any height and is often used as the last stitch to create a smooth and even round or row.

1. To make a slip stitch: first put the hook through the work, yarn round hook.

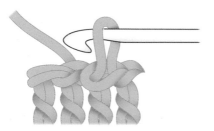

2. Pull the yarn through both the work and through the loop on the hook at the same time, so you will have one loop on the hook.

Working into top of stitch

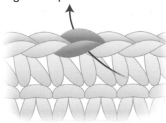

Unless otherwise directed, insert the hook under both of the two loops on top of the stitch – this is the standard technique.

Working into front loop of stitch (flo)

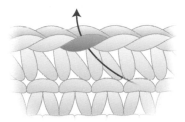

To work into the front loop of a stitch, pick up the front loop from underneath at the front of the work.

Working into back loop of stitch (blo)

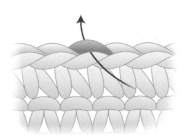

To work into the back loop of the stitch, insert the hook between the front and the back loop, picking up the back loop from the front of the work.

Double crochet (dc)

1. Insert the hook into your work, yarn round hook and pull the yarn through the work only. You will then have two loops on the hook.

2. Yarn round hook again and pull through the two loops on the hook. You will then have one loop on the hook.

Joining new yarn

If using double crochet to join in a new yarn, insert the hook as normal into the stitch, using the original yarn, and pull a loop through. Drop the old yarn and pick up the new yarn. Wrap the new yarn round the hook and pull it through the two loops on the hook.

Half treble crochet (htr)

1. Before inserting the hook into the work, wrap the yarn round the hook and put the hook through the work with the yarn wrapped around.

2. Yarn round hook again and pull through the first loop on the hook. You now have three loops on the hook.

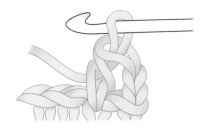

3. Yarn round hook and pull the yarn through all three loops. You will be left with one loop on the hook.

Treble crochet (tr)

1. Before inserting the hook into the work, wrap the yarn round the hook. Put the hook through the work with the yarn wrapped around, yarn round hook again and pull through the first loop on the hook. You now have three loops on the hook.

2. Yarn round hook again, pull the yarn through the first two loops on the hook. You now have two loops on the hook.

3. Pull the yarn through two loops again. You will be left with one loop on the hook.

Double Treble (dtr)

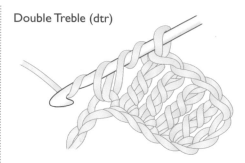

This stitch is longer than treble and requires more wraps of the yarn. It creates a very open fabric. Yarn round hook twice, insert the hook in the stitch or chain, yarn round hook, pull the yarn through the work (4 loops on hook), [yarn round hook, pull yarn through first two loops on the hook] twice (2 loops on hook), yarn round hook, pull yarn through last two loops (1 loop on hook).

Triple treble (trtr)

Triple trebles are "tall" stitches and are an extension on the basic treble stitch. They need a turning chain of 5 chains.

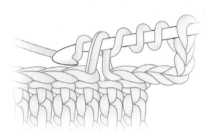

1. Yarn round hook three times, insert the hook into the stitch or space.

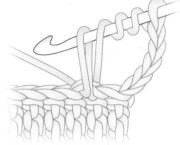

2. Yarn round hook, pull the yarn through the work (5 loops on hook).

3. Yarn round hook, pull the yarn through the first 2 loops on the hook (4 loops on hook).

4. Yarn round hook, pull the yarn through the first 2 loops on the hook (3 loops on hook).

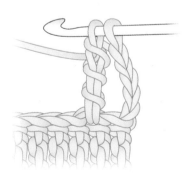

5. Yarn round hook, pull the yarn through the first 2 loops on the hook (2 loops on hook).

6. Yarn round hook, pull the yarn through 2 loops on the hook (1 loop on hook). One triple treble completed.

Increasing

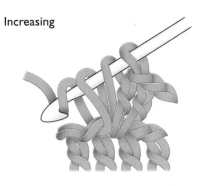

Make two or three stitches into one stitch or space from the previous row. The illustration shows a two-stitch treble crochet increase being made.

Blocking

Crochet can tend to curl so to make flat pieces stay flat you may need to block them. Pin the piece out to the correct size and shape on the ironing board, then press or steam gently (depending on the type of yarn) and allow to dry completely.

Decreasing

You can decrease by either missing the next stitch and continuing to crochet, or by crocheting two or more stitches together. The basic technique for crocheting stitches together is the same, no matter which stitch you are using. The following examples show dc2tog, htr2tog, and tr2tog.

Double crochet two stitches together (dc2tog)

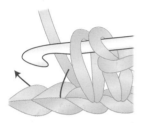

1. Insert the hook into your work, yarn round hook and pull the yarn through the work. You will then have two loops on the hook.

2. Yarn round hook again and pull through the two loops on the hook. You will then have one loop on the hook.

Half treble crochet two stitches together (htr2tog)

1. Yarn round hook, insert hook into next stitch, yarn round hook, draw yarn through. You now have three loops on the hook.

2. Yarn round hook, insert hook into next stitch, yarn round hook, draw yarn through. This leaves five loops on the hook.

3. Draw the yarn through all five loops on the hook. You will then have one loop on the hook.

Treble crochet two stitches together (tr2tog)

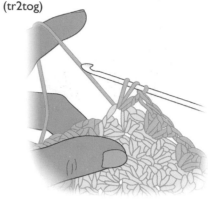

1. Yarn round hook, insert the hook into the next space, yarn round hook, pull the yarn through the work (3 loops on hook).

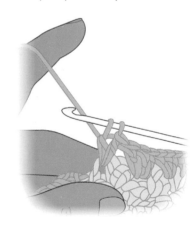

2. Yarn round hook, pull the yarn through two loops on the hook (2 loops on hook).

3. Yarn round hook, insert the hook into the next space.

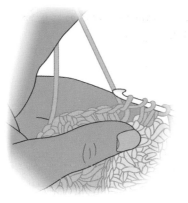

4. Yarn round hook, pull the yarn through the work (4 loops on hook).

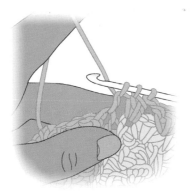

5. Yarn round hook, pull the yarn through 2 loops on the hook (3 loops on hook).

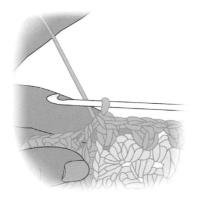

6. Yarn round hook, pull the yarn through all 3 loops on the hook (1 loop on hook). One tr2tog (decrease) made.

Weaving in yarn ends

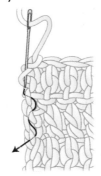

It is important to weave in the tail ends of the yarn so that they are secure and your crochet won't unravel. Thread a tapestry needle with the tail end of yarn. On the wrong side, take the needle through the crochet one stitch down on the edge, then take it through the stitches, working in a gentle zigzag. Work through 4 or 5 stitches then return in the opposite direction. Remove the needle, pull the crochet gently to stretch it, and trim the end.

Sewing up

Sewing up crochet fabric can be done in many ways, but using a whip stitch is the easiest. However, you will be able to see the stitches clearly, so use a matching yarn. Lay the two pieces to be joined next to each other with right sides facing upward. Secure the yarn to one piece. Insert the needle into the front of one piece of fabric, then up from the back of the adjoining fabric. Repeat along the seam.

Sewing on a bead

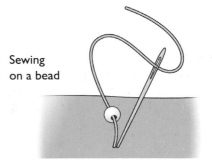

Bring the thread up through the fabric then thread on the bead. Take the thread over the bead and back down through the fabric.

Sewing on a button

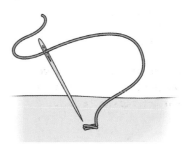

1. Mark the place where you want the button to go. Push the needle up from the back of the fabric and sew a few stitches over and over in this place.

2. Now bring the needle up through one of the holes in the button. Push the needle back down through the second hole and through the fabric. Bring it back up through the first hole. Repeat this five or six times. If there are four holes in the button, use all four of them to make a cross pattern. Make sure that you keep the stitches close together under the middle of the button.

CROCHET STITCH CONVERSION CHART

Crochet stitches are worked in the same way in both the UK and the USA, but the stitch names are not the same and identical names are used for different stitches. Below is a list of the UK terms used in this book, and the equivalent US terms.

UK TERM	US TERM
double crochet (dc)	single crochet (sc)
half treble (htr)	half double crochet (hdc)
treble (tr)	double crochet (dc)
double treble (dtr)	treble (tr)
triple treble (trtr)	double treble (dtr)
quadruple treble (qtr)	triple treble (trtr)
tension	gauge
yarn round hook (yrh)	yarn over hook (yoh)

SUPPLIERS

USA

Knitting Fever Inc.
PO Box 336
315 Bayview Avenue
Amityville, NY 11701
www.knittingfever.com

Lion Brand Yarns
Tel: +1-800-258 YARN (9276)
Online sales and store locator on website
www.lionbrand.com

Westminster Fibers
165 Ledge Street
Nashua, NH 03060
Tel: +1-800-445-9276
www.westminsterfibers.com

Accessories:
A.C. Moore
Stores nationwide
Tel: +1-888-226-6673
www.acmoore.com

Hobby Lobby
Online store and stores nationwide
www.hobbylobby.com

Michaels
Stores nationwide
Tel: +1-800-642-4235
www.michaels.com

Canada
Diamond Yarn
155 Martin Ross Avenue, Unit 3
Toronto, ON
M3J 2L9
Tel: +1-416-736-6111
www.diamondyarn.com

Patons
320 Livingstone Avenue South, Box 40
Listowel, ON, N4W 3HD3
Tel: +1-888-368-8401
www.yarninspirations.com

Westminster Fibers
10 Roybridge Gate, Suite 200
Vaughan, ON
L4H 3M8
Tel: +1-800-263-2354
www.westminsterfibers.com

UK
Debbie Bliss Yarns
Designer Yarns Ltd
Units 8–10 Newbridge Industrial Estate
Pitt Street, Keighly
West Yorkshire BD21 4PQ
Tel: +44 (0)1535 664222
www.debbieblissonline.com

Deramores
Online store only
Tel: +44 (0)800 488 0708
www.deramores.com

John Lewis
Retail stores and online
www.johnlewis.com
Telephone numbers of local stores on website
Tel: +44 (0)3456 049049

Rowan
Rowan Yarns
Green Lane Mill
Holmfirth
West Yorkshire HD9 2DX
Tel: +44 (0)1484 681881
www.knitrowan.com

Sirdar
Sirdar Spinning Ltd
Flanshaw Lane
Wakefield
West Yorkshire WF2 9ND
Tel: +44 (0)1924 231682
www.sirdar.co.uk

Australia
Black Sheep Wool 'n' Wares
Tel: +61 (0)2 6779 1196
www.blacksheepwool.com.au

Creative Images Crafts
PO Box 106
Hastings
VIC 3915
Tel: +61 (0)3 5979 1555

INDEX

A

abbreviations 8
animals
    Grey Rabbit 114–117
    Little Crab 28–29
    Parrot 20–21
    Pussy Cat 78–81
    Spider 106–107
Apple 76–77
Arrow Quiver 50–51

B

Basket 74–75
beads, sewing on 125
beards
    Pirate's Beard 14
    Wizard's Beard 112–113
blocking 123
buttons, sewing on 125

C

chain (ch) 119
chain ring 119
chain space (ch-sp) 120
Chest Plate 36–37
Cobweb Collar 104–105
collars
    Cobweb Collar 104–105
    Snowflake Collar 42–43
Corsage 59
Cowboy Carl (or Carla) 62–69
craft wire 8
cuffs
    Icicle Cuffs 44–45
    Superhero Cuffs 34–35
    Viking Cuffs 92–93
    Wrist Guards 52–53

D

decreasing 124–125
double crochet (dc) 121
double treble (dtr) 122

E

equipment 8
Eye Patch 15

F

Fairy Wings 60–61
Flower Garland 56–57
Forest Fairy 54–61

G

Grey Rabbit 114–117

H

hair
    Mermaid's Hair 24–25
    Rapunzel's Hair 96–97
half treble crochet (htr) 121
hats
    Cowboy Hat 64–65
    Mask 32–33
    Peaked Hat 48–49
    Pussy Cat Hat 80
    Rabbit Hat 116
    Tricorn Hat 16–17
    Viking Helmet 88–89
    Witch's Hat 102–103
    Wizard's Hat 110–111
Holster 66–67
Hooded Cape 72–73
hook
    holding the hook 118
    sizes 8
    yarn around hook 119
Horn Headdress 84–85

I

Icicle Cuffs 44–45
increasing 123

L

Little Crab 28–29
Little Mermaid 22–29

M

magic ring 119
Magic Unicorn 82–85
Mask 32–33

P

Parrot 20–21
Peaked Hat 48–49
Pete the Pirate 12–21
Pussy Cat 78–81

R

Rabbit Hat 116
Rapunzel 94–99
Red Riding Hood 70–77
Robin Hood 46–53
rounds, working in 119, 120
rows, making 120

S

sewing up crochet 125
Sheriff's Badge 68–69
Shrug 98–99
Skull & Crossbones Motif 18–19
slip knot 118
slip stitch (ss) 120
Snow Queen 38–45
Snowflake Collar 42–43
Snowflake Crown 40–41
Spider 106–107
stitch conversion chart 126
stitch marker 8
stitch techniques
    working into back loop of stitch 121
    working into front loop of stitch 121
    working into top of stitch 121
stitches
    double crochet (dc) 121
    double treble (dtr) 122
    half treble crochet (htr) 121
    slip stitch (ss) 120
    treble crochet (tr) 122
    triple treble (trtr) 123
Superhero 30–37

T

tails
    Magic Unicorn Tail 85
    Mermaid Tail 26–27
    Pussy Cat Tail 81
    Rabbit Tail 117
tapestry needle 8
techniques 118–125
Thor's Hammer 90–91
treble crochet (tr) 122
Tricorn Hat 16–17
triple treble (trtr) 123

V

Vigo the Viking 86–93

W

Wicked Witch 100–107
Wily Wizard 108–113
Witch's Hat 102–103
Wizard's Hat 110–111
Wrist Guards 52–53

Y

yarns 8
    holding the yarn 118
    joining new yarn 121
    small quantity 8
    weaving in yarn ends 125

ACKNOWLEDGMENTS

Compiling this book from patterns that were originally made just to be worn and played with has been such a fantastic experience. It's amazing that we can share them with other people and hopefully they'll be played with just as much too.

I'd like to thank Cindy Richards and Penny Craig at CICO for seeing the potential in what was essentially a pile of bonkers, woollen things; Rachel Atkinson for her sterling (and often challenging) work as editor, interpreting some of my frankly made up crochet techniques; and Zoe Clements for pattern checking so thoroughly.

I have to thank Neil, my husband, for encouraging me to write my patterns down in the first place, my beasts and nephews for all the inspiration – they are my muses – my horrible twin sister for the infernal unicorn, and the rest of my family for all their support. A special shout out has to go to the amazing Susannah for all her positivity and input, and an even bigger thank you to Freya for helping with all the girly things and trying stuff on.